Formalism and Functionalism in Linguistics

T0386202

This volume is a concise introduction to the lively ongoing debate between formalist and functionalist approaches to the study of language. The book grounds its comparisons between the two in both historical and contemporary contexts where, broadly speaking, formalists' focus on structural relationships and idealized linguistic data contrasts with functionalists' commitment to analyzing real language used as a communicative tool. The book highlights key sub-varieties, proponents, and critiques of each respective approach. It concludes by comparing formalist versus functionalist contributions in three domains of linguistic research: in the analysis of specific grammatical constructions; in the study of language acquisition; and in interdisciplinary research on the origins of language. Taken together, the volume opens insight into an important tension in linguistic theory and provides students and scholars with a more nuanced understanding of the structure of the discipline of modern linguistics.

Margaret Thomas is Professor of Linguistics in the Department of Slavic and Eastern Languages and Literatures at Boston College, USA.

Formalism and Functionalism in Linguistics

The Engineer and the Collector

Margaret Thomas

NEW YORK AND LONDON

First published 2020
by Routledge
605 Third Avenue, New York, NY 10017

and by Routledge
2 Park Square, Milton Park, Abingdon, Oxon, OX14 4RN

First issued in paperback 2021

Routledge is an imprint of the Taylor & Francis Group, an informa business

© 2020 Taylor & Francis

Library of Congress Cataloging-in-Publication Data
A catalog record for this book has been requested

ISBN 13: 978-0-367-78784-4 (pbk)
ISBN 13: 978-1-138-31611-9 (hbk)

Typeset in Times New Roman
by Apex CoVantage, LLC

Contents

Acknowledgments

I am grateful to Boston College students of linguistics who enrolled in the inaugural version of the course *Formalism and functionalism*. They worked through this material with me, adding a lot to my understanding. I also thank my Research Assistants Camila Loforte, whose diligence and resourcefulness improved the text on every level and Seung Hwan Kim, whose help with matters large and small was invaluable at the last stages of completion of this project. Editor Elysse Preposi was a pleasure to work with, as was the rest of the Routledge production team. Finally, I thank the anonymous reviewers of the manuscript for their thoughtful critique.

Introduction

Readers of this book probably do not need to be introduced to the observation that human language displays intricate patterns, on many levels of organization. They probably already recognize that languages both resemble and differ from each other, and, moreover, that language is characteristic of our species, so that without it human culture would be unimaginable. It is likely that readers assume from the start that language is a complex multi-dimensional phenomenon. Many, but perhaps not all, identify linguistics as the scientific study of language.

On the other hand, there is much that readers of this book may not share as students of language. Some of that diversity of outlook derives from sub-specialization, because (for example) historical linguistics does not overlap very much with speech pathology, nor does dialectology with neurolinguistics. Some of it derives from exposure to different language data: one linguist works within the tradition of Germanic language scholarship, while another does field research in Melanesia. Moreover, linguists and linguists-in-training adopt different stances along theoretical continua. Following in the style of their education, and according to their personal intellectual dispositions, they find their own sweet spots within all manner of controversies.

The diversity of sub-specialization, exposure, and stance (among other factors) keeps modern linguistics lively. This book addresses one particularly lively dimension of difference among contemporary linguists, the upshot of which is under-appreciated. That difference comes to the surface in debate between 'formalist' and 'functionalist' approaches to the study of language. Not all linguistic research can be identified with either formalism or functionalism, nor does every individual proposal or claim fall exhaustively within one of the two camps. Nevertheless, achieving a clear understanding of what is at stake in the tension between formalism and functionalism is invaluable. In particular, it helps make sense of the competing claims that students of linguistics encounter and enlarges their sense of the scope of the discipline. It is not my goal to judge the outcome of competition between formalism and functionalism or to try to resolve the tension between them. Rather, my hope is that by learning to recognize the traits of formalism versus functionalism, readers will be better able to assess (in)consistency in a body of work and better able to tailor their own analyses of language data to whatever theoretical commitments they make.

This book is organized as follows. Chapter 1 points out some defining features of formalism and of functionalism, illustrating them with a look at two recent books which introduce the public to modern linguistic research, one from each side of the debate. Chapter 2 provides some historical context to modern formalism and functionalism. Chapters 3 and 4 are sibling chapters, with the first surveying contemporary formalist linguistics from the late 1950s onward and the second depicting representative schools and scholars of contemporary functionalist linguistics over the same interval. Chapter 5 depicts formalism and functionalism in action, showing how each has been brought to bear on three issues: the analysis of particular grammatical phenomena (word order; transitivity); research on child language learning; and the fraught question of the origin of human language. Chapter 6 juxtaposes formalism against functionalism and vice versa from several standpoints, analyzing different positions the two have taken up relative to each other. Chapter 7 concludes.

In the interest of conciseness, I have excluded two plausible topics from this text. One is research on phonology, as almost all the examples and discussion included here address morphosyntax. Several commentators have remarked that there is more coherence across formalist and functionalist work in phonology than in other domains (Haspelmath 2000; Curnow 2002; Carnie & Mendoza-Denton 2003). I have therefore opted to focus on issues where the two approaches are in sharper contrast. Another neglected topic is the phenomena of grammaticalization, the process by which, over time, a referential lexical item shifts to take on a functional (or grammatical) role. There are two reasons why, reluctantly, I excluded discussion of grammaticalization: first, because it has a very high profile in functionalist accounts of language change, while it is more peripheral to formalism and addressed in a more diffuse manner. This imbalance complicates comparison. Second, Fischer (2007; see also Fischer, Rosenbach & Stein 2000) gives a rich book-length treatment of grammaticalization, managing to balance formalist and functionalist perspectives. Fischer's text should be fully accessible to readers of the current book, and I recommend it as follow-up reading. I would also recommend Newmeyer (1998), which offers both depth and scope of treatment of formalism versus functionalism from the perspective of a committed but open minded formalist.

References

Carnie, Andrew and Norma Mendoza-Denton. (2003). 'Functionalism is/n't formalism: An interactive review of Darnell et al. (1999)'. *Journal of Linguistics* 39: 373–389.

Curnow, Timothy J. (2002). [Review of the book *Functionalism and formalism in linguistics*]. *Studies in Language* 26(2): 505–512.

Fischer, Olga. (2007). *Morphosyntactic change: Functional and formal perspectives*. Oxford: Oxford University Press.

Fischer, Olga, Anette Rosenbach, and Dieter Stein (Eds.). (2000). *Pathways of change: Grammaticalization in English*. Amsterdam/Philadelphia: John Benjamins Press.

Haspelmath, Martin. (2000). 'Why can't we talk to each other?' [Review of the book *Language form and language function*]. *Lingua* 110: 235–255.

Newmeyer, Frederick J. (1998). *Language form and language function*. Cambridge, MA: MIT Press.

1 Defining 'Formalism' and 'Functionalism'

1.1 Starting Out

The terms 'formalism' and 'functionalism' name two contrasting stances that some language scholars assume, sometimes explicitly, sometimes only implicitly. Distinctively formalist versus functionalist approaches are recognizable in (for example) how linguists gather, analyze, and account for language data, how they design their research programs, and how they define the scope of linguistic inquiry. Employment of these two labels is relatively new, as is the notion that they are rivals within the same conceptual space. Nevertheless, each has a line of descent in the history of linguistics up to the present day. Chapter 1 provides some preliminary descriptions of what the two terms stand for. The remainder of this text illustrates, elaborates on, and sometimes challenges those descriptions.

One might start by pointing out what 'formalism' and 'functionalism' are *not*. They are not necessarily self-consciously designated categories with relatively clear boundaries, like 'Darwinian' and 'anti-Darwinian'. Transporting the issue into a different domain by way of illustration, 'formalism' and 'functionalism' have some of the properties of informal labels like 'progressive' or 'centrist' as those terms are used in political discussions. One could, for instance, dispute whether a particular policy counts as truly 'progressive' despite its supporters' claim to that characterization. One could also argue whether another policy is or isn't 'centrist' regardless of whether proponents position it on a continuum between 'progressive' and 'centrist'; and many policies may not be recognizably either progressive or centrist. Nevertheless, these categories still serve a purpose, as do 'formalism' and 'functionalism'. They help organize a complex, multi-dimensional, conceptual landscape and sharpen our perceptual and analytic powers.

A second important caveat, and a second way in which formalism and functionalism differ from categories like 'Darwinian' versus 'anti-Darwinian', is that they are not necessarily symmetrical relative to each other. Formalism brings into view language phenomena which functionalism discounts or ignores and vice versa. The two approaches do sometimes address the same issue only to arrive at complementary conclusions. However, there are also instances where formalism and functionalism each independently pursues an objective, employing assumptions and conceptual tools that the other would consider alien or extraneous. In this sense, formalism and functionalism do not always compete side by side. Sometimes their contributions to our understanding of human language can be coordinated. At other times they are simply incommensurable.

1.2 Defining the Terms

Curnow (2002: 506) quipped that formalists are scholars who are sure they know what 'functionalism' is, whereas functionalists are those who are confident that they can readily define 'formalism'. The remark is light-hearted, but it calls attention to the difficulty each side may encounter in identifying a coherent core within its own practices and intellectual commitments. We will start by taking a step away from language to consider the sense of the words 'formalism' and 'functionalism' in other disciplines.

Formalism in general—in art, architecture, literary criticism, logic, philosophy—emphasizes the structure and organization of the object of analysis, sometimes conceived as extracted out of its overlying material presentation. Formal logic translates a sentence into a skeleton of basic symbolic elements, removing whatever cannot be so represented. Formal literary criticism highlights the linguistic material and component parts of a text rather than its reception or historical role. Formal(ist) architecture is characterized by monumental symmetry, precise alignment of iterated geometric shapes, nested angles, subdued colors. Although the term takes on different senses in different domains, those approaches or styles labeled 'formal' typically look inward to the shape and organization of a phenomenon, often by abstracting away from its surface appearance and its relationships with neighboring phenomena.

'Functionalism', on the other hand, emphasizes the roles that phenomena play in their larger contexts, sublimating structure to function. In the first half of the twentieth century, functionalism in sociology turned the study of families, cultural practices, and institutions toward investigation of how these elements of a society contributed (or not) to the community's integrity and stability overall. In architecture, the American Louis Sullivan (1856–1924) famously asserted that 'form ever follows function' (1896: 406), hyperbolically depicting that claim as 'the pervading law of all things organic and inorganic'. Sullivan's aphorism, conventionally cited as 'form follows function', was adopted by designers who deliberately shaped buildings according to their local environments and the uses to which people put them. For example, rather than flattening a hillside to accommodate the footprint of a library, functionalist architects may build the library into the hill; they may round the corners of an office tower on a busy street to facilitate the flow of pedestrians around it; they may extend the overhang above an entrance to a house to protect owners from the rain as they fumble for their keys, even as that extension interrupts the harmony of the building's facade. In these ways, functionalism not only incorporates but prizes asymmetry and even idiosyncrasy as a response to external, contextually imposed demands.

Overall, then, it may be fair to say that for formalists, form transcends function, or at least that they prioritize form over content or context. For functionalists, form derives from function in the sense that the role a phenomenon fills within its environment determines its internal structure. In linguistics, formalists analyze language as a system shaped by formal, structural rules. Formalists take for granted that close articulation of those rules (or constraints, principles, etc.) is the central task of language scholars. Fischer (2007: 54) wrote that for formalists 'the *system* of grammar [is] more important as an object of study than the actual language data' (emphasis in the original). Therefore, formalists characteristically look inward to explain linguistic phenomena: in some instances, this means that they explain a newly-observed fact of language according to how it fits within the configuration of already-established formal linguistic facts. In other instances, formalists look inward to explain facts according to their status in language change or acquisition. Functionalists, on the other hand, prioritize language data and prize detailed, contextualized, records of its use. They characteristically look outside language for explanations, under the assumption that languages are what they are because of the exigencies of human communication and cognition, or because of the external cultural environment in which language is used. To functionalists, the central task is to define how the shape of language data is connected to its communicative purposes and to human cognitive resources.

1.3 The Engineer and the Collector

From these bare-bones definitions of our two key terms, it is clear that each is not the simple converse of the other. Although in some instances formalism and functionalism do look like paired opposites, it is more accurate to conceive of them as heterogeneous assemblies of traits which are independent of each other and only sometimes match up as mirror images across the formalist/functionalist divide. At the risk of over-simplification, the Appendix to this book compiles some of those traits, contrasting in one column the purported features of (at least some versions of) formalism to the purported features of (at least some versions of) functionalism in the opposing column.

It is important to grasp, first, that the contents of the Appendix are not a summary, but only a collection of entry points; and, second, that the entries in the two lists characterize the two terms rather than define them, since not all specimens of formalism or functionalism exhibit all traits. An analogy may help. Consider two lists that informally assemble the characteristics of animals versus plants: for animals, 'can move', 'eats and digests', 'reproduces sexually'; for plants, 'green color', 'has roots', 'requires sun'. The lists would have to be read with the understanding that, in fact, not every animal reproduces sexually, while many plants do so; and that there certainly exist both plants that are not green (e.g., *Monotropa uniflora*, also know as 'ghost pipe') and animals that are green (e.g., parrots). Analogously, formalists characteristically embrace abstraction, while functionalists are characteristically at home carrying out deep analyses of particulars and specific cases. But sometimes the converse relationships may hold, and sometimes neither abstraction nor a focus on particulars is relevant to work that is otherwise recognizably formalist or functionalist.

The contents of the Appendix will be filled out, explored, and sometimes disrupted, in the remainder of this text. In the meantime, it may be useful to fuse each of these sets of traits into two images, each one representing metaphorically the approach to analysis of language data taken by formalists versus functionalists. Representing formalism, picture an engineer's framework for a building silhouetted against the sky, comprised of idealized geometrical shapes iteratively embedded within each other. That framework is the bare skeleton that underlies a structure, stripped of its recognizable accoutrements such as plaster, paint, woodwork, and all manner of surface treatment. It is modular in the sense that its sub-parts can be separated, analyzed as independent units, and assembled piecemeal to comprise the whole. A viewer is struck by the symmetry of multiple parallel lines and angles and by the abstractness of the total ensemble relative to the daily experience of encountering walls, doors, or stairways. Likewise, formalist linguists foreground the skeleton of a language, the patterned substructures of its parts, and the immaterial, sometimes only hypothesized, relationships that hold among those parts in a manner that looks beyond how we encounter them in their normal working environments.

Representing functionalism, picture what was called in the eighteenth century a 'cabinet of curiosity', a miniaturized precursor to the modern museum of natural history. Returning travelers would assemble for display their collected mementos from abroad, sometimes variously comprising a shell, a rock, a taxidermy specimen, a human artifact, the fragment of a bone, a preserved flower or insect. Typically, each sample sits in its own box or enclosed niche or on a shelf or drawer comprised of multiple small spaces each dedicated to a single item. Because the logic behind the juxtaposition of items is not necessarily obvious, this style of exhibition discourages facile generalizations. Instead, it seems to communicate that every specimen is worthy of attention and holds a unique place in the total collection. A viewer moves freely among them, speculating on the role played by each item in the human or natural ecology that produced it. Likewise, functionalist linguists observe and curate language phenomena, inspecting them for evidence of how they interact and making sense of their material properties with reference to the totality of the superstructure which, together, they constitute.

In the terms of this metaphor, a formalist scholar of language resembles a linguistic engineer, who designs models of the inner framework that supports human language. A functionalist language scholar resembles a linguistic collector or curator, who scrutinizes samples of human languages with the goal of understanding how they accomplish their communicative roles. The metaphorical images of engineer versus collector probably overstate differences between formalists and functionalists. However, these images have the virtue of not forcing the one into a mirror-image mold of the other, since what an engineer accomplishes is not undone, nor is it performed in reverse, by what a collector accomplishes. The two images have the additional virtue of problematizing any facile initiative to combine formalism with functionalism. Although the work of an engineer and of a collector are not incompatible *per se*, to harmonize the two in any meaningful way without undermining their differences would require cautious and respectful treatment of them both and deep understanding of the attributes of each one.

1.4 Two Examples

Two recent non-technical books that introduce linguistics to the public exemplify contrasting formalist versus functionalist approaches in modern study of language. The two texts differ starkly—in their goals, their rhetoric, and their style of argumentation. One is short, one long. One author writes from the center of modern formalism; the other author's functionalism is eccentric. Both books are mostly taken up with exposition of their authors' positions, with only one giving much attention to the opposing point of view. However, they are comparable in the sense that each takes a thoroughgoing, uncompromising stance that sharply contrasts with the stance taken by the other. Surveying them side by side provides a useful microcosm of how one variety of modern formalism differs from one variety of modern functionalism, with the two situated intellectually so that the distance between them is large.

Andrea Moro's *Impossible Languages* (2016) represents a formalist point of view. Affiliated with the Institute for Advanced Study at the University of Pavia, Moro (b. 1962) is a linguist and neuroscientist whose work has been consistently informed by generative theory (e.g., Chomsky 1995). He begins by fearlessly announcing that 'To define the class of possible languages: this is the ultimate aim of linguistics' (p. 1). Moro argues that there are biologically based limits to the structure of a human language, which make sense of the notion of an 'impossible' language. An impossible language would be one that could be shown not to share the 'unique, intricate set of principles with relatively little variation, producing a surprising constellation of properties' (p. 5) asserted to be attested in all languages. Moro's book is an extended argument that, in fact, impossible languages do not exist because those 'unique, intricate' principles necessarily constrain the structure of every natural human language. Moreover, principles of language structure cannot, according to Moro, be discovered on the basis of simple observation of the surface forms of sounds and words. Rather, they are derived by theory-driven analysis of what child language learners know about the structure of language, despite the absence or inadequacy of evidence in their environment that could lead them to that knowledge, that is, despite 'the poverty of the stimulus' (Chomsky 1980).

Moro's approach to the study of language is consummately formalist. A brief aside on page 2 spells this out. He acknowledges that alongside their formal and physical properties, 'human languages must be endowed with other general properties that make them not only possible but usable'. He specifies that those properties include the capacity to carry meaning and serve communicative ends—then he pivots to remark flatly that 'These properties are trivial' (p. 2). With that in place, Moro's text goes on to exhibit many of the hallmarks of formalism. For example, the linguistic data Moro cites is highly stylized, in the sense that he engineers it to demonstrate specific language properties rather than to depict actual speakers' actual usage (e.g., *Who do you think that Mary wants to describe themselves?*, p. 23; *This fact that John runs surprises me*, p. 29). Moro identifies these data dichotomously as either syntactically well-formed or ill-formed, without reference to any context of their use in speech or writing. It is also significant that Moro consistently makes bold synthetic claims, then seeks support for those claims in highly abstract analyses of language data. For instance, he argues that the complex syntactic properties of all languages can be attributed to the operation of two functions, namely recursion and locality (pp. 34ff). Later, Moro introduces experimental evidence that the acoustic waves generated by speech correlate with the electromagnetic waves generated by silent reading. On this basis, he speculates that recursion and locality can be united in being derived from a code in which sound waves and brain waves converge, amounting to an unexpected 'unification of the physical properties of language with its formal ones' (p. 96).

Moro's idealization of linguistic data and his facility with abstraction are recognizably formalist in spirit. The specifically generativist orientation within the formalism of *Impossible languages* is evident as well, for example, in that Moro presupposes the existence of a cognitive faculty specific to human language (p. 59) and in that he consistently compares the work of linguists, their methodology, and their results to those in the natural sciences, including chemistry (p. 17), immunology (p. 19), mathematics (p. 27), neurobiology (pp. 45–59), and physics (pp. 63–70). It is also characteristic of generativist formalism to privilege the ease and speed with which children come into language as an especially consequential source of insight into the nature of human language (pp. 13–15)—or, in Moro's terms, into the non-existence of impossible languages.

In these ways, Moro's approach and the focus of his project itself—to define what would count as an impossible language—are demonstrably formalist, the work of a linguist-engineer. Moro's book sharply contrasts with Daniel L. Everett's 2012 *Language, the Cultural Tool*. Everett (b. 1951) is a controversial American anthropological linguist whose research on Amazonian languages, especially Pirahã (spoken by a few hundred people in the center of the Brazilian Amazon basin) has attracted attention in both academic and popular media. As with Moro, Everett's title establishes his theme: 'language is a tool *for us* and designed *by us*. And *we set the rules* for the interpretation and use of language' (p. 124; emphasis in the original). Not all functionalists would agree with the precise stance he takes, but Everett is still as recognizable as a functionalist as Moro is as a formalist.

Everett devotes more attention to the opposing point of view than does Moro, so that *Language, the Cultural Tool* is about three times the length of *Impossible Languages*. Everett's book has met with more public attention than Moro's in the non-specialist press (Radford 2012; Tomlinson 2012; Williams 2012) and from linguists (McWhorter 2012; Enfield 2013). It ranges widely over many topics in linguistics and linguistic anthropology of high interest to the general public, including the Sapir-Whorf Hypothesis; color and kinship terms; child language learning; animal communication; garden path sentences; the foibles of prescriptive grammar; creole languages; differences between icon, index, and symbol; rare articulatory gestures like linguolabials, ejectives, or implosives; and so forth. Everett exuberantly displays this diverse collection of language concepts, claims, and practices in the service of illustrating his theme of the mutual influence between language and culture. In this, Everett's emphasis is less on language as a general human phenomenon as it is on specific languages and their associations with specific groups: kinship terms and incest taboos in Hawaiian (pp. 246–248); invention versus cultural borrowing in Sequoya's creation of the Cherokee syllabary (pp. 273–276); default feminine gender marking on nouns in the Amazonian language Banawá in the context of segregation by sex in Banawá culture (pp. 207–210).

The centerpiece of Everett's collection of linguistic marvels, however, is Pirahã language and culture. His presentation is based on deep personal experience with speakers of Pirahã, gleaned from years of living among them. Throughout the book, he uses the features of Pirahã to illustrate the nexus of language, cognition, and culture. Everett reports, for instance, that the Pirahã language lacks words that mark temporal and aspectual differences: verbs don't encode either the time reference of an event (*ate dinner; will eat dinner*) or its character as ongoing or completed (*was eating; has eaten*). He sees this as directly reflecting Pirahã speakers' radical here-and-now cognitive orientation, which entails a lack of conceptualization of the passage of time. They live in 'a society in which members sleep, eat, hunt, fish, and gather without regard to time of day, day of the week, week of the month, or month of the year' (p. 269). Likewise, Everett comments on the extensive practices of reciprocal physical grooming among the Pirahã, which co-exist in their culture with a relative dearth of phatic utterances, that is, the 'linguistic grooming' that (for example) speakers of English engage in with small-talk exchanges like 'How are you?'/'Fine, and you?' or 'Bye now'/'See you later' (pp. 236–239).

Everett interprets these observations as evidence for how linguistic form conforms to culturally-embedded linguistic function. His treatment of data is similarly functionalist, on several levels. He provides long passages of transliterated Pirahã reproducing connected speech (pp. 278–279; 295–297), introduced with the specifics of the who, when, where, and why of the attested language. Everett's 'bottom-up' inductivist stance is even inscribed in the famous story of how he first approached the Pirahã people, adverted to in *Language, the Cultural Tool* and fully developed in Everett (2008). Everett arrived in Brazil as a missionary whose goal was to learn Pirahã for the purpose of Christian evangelization. He had had some training in applied linguistics to prepare him to translate the Bible. As time passed, however, Everett came to appreciate and value Pirahã culture, so that his orientation shifted from religious conversion to the effort to understand both their language and their culture. He then acquired the intellectual tools to do advanced linguistic research by completing a doctorate in linguistics at the University of Campinas in São Paulo. In Everett's biography as in his intellectual priorities, the data came first and then the theory followed to help make sense of the data, rather than vice versa.

To sharpen the contrast between Moro and Everett, it may help to assess their treatments of a topic that comes up in both books: localization of language in the brain. Both scholars give compressed versions of the famous story of French surgeon and physical anthropologist Paul Broca's 1861 autopsy of a man with aphasia, which led Broca to identify the physical locus of human language in the third frontal convolution of the left hemisphere ('Broca's area': Moro 2016: 48–49; Everett 2012: 74–75). Both also caution readers against too literal a version of the claim that grammar resides exhaustively in a single identifiable location. But Moro and Everett present the complexities that attend localization of language in the brain quite differently. Moro suggests that rather than being the seat of the language faculty, Broca's area may resemble a hub airport in the world of air travel: not a destination in itself, but the crucial place where many lines cross in a multiplex system. Moro narrates a series of neurolinguistic experiments which compared blood flow to Broca's area when subjects tried to learn one of two facets of an invented language: rules that were recursive, and which resemble those of natural languages, versus rules that were linear and non-recursive (e.g., 'form a question by inverting the order of words in a sentence'), which presumably resemble hypothesized impossible languages (pp. 55–59). The results showed increasing involvement in Broca's area as subjects learned recursive rules and decreasing involvement as they learned linear, 'impossible', rules. Although Moro warns that his results do not resolve the exact role of Broca's area, he asserts that those results do show that 'the distinction between possible and impossible languages is embodied in the brain', a finding which denies 'the alleged arbitrary, cultural, and conventional character of human languages' (p. 59).

In these ways, Moro introduces the classic notion of brain localization; retreats from its strong version; then reports an empirical study that assumes a nuanced relevance for Broca's area. That study employs recognizably formalist methods and constructs. Its results confirm Moro's formalist commitments.

Everett likewise adheres to his functionalist commitments. He frames brain localization research in a more skeptical light, emphasizing that 'the evidence is far from clear' (p. 73) and labeling the reputation of Broca's area as 'part of urban and academic folklore' (p. 74). Everett lists five objections to investing Broca's area with a unique linguistic role but stops short of denying that it has any independent existence or relevance to language: 'everyone agrees that there are regions of the brain involved in language' (p. 75). He goes on to cite several studies showing that when blind persons read Braille, they activate parts of the brain associated with the processing of visual stimuli (p. 76). He interprets this finding as evidence that, first, the external fact of being blind bears on brain function, and second, that language processing is not confined to identified language centers. Everett also refers to research which reported that children struggling to learn to read grow new brain material in as little as six months of intensive training (p. 78), a finding he takes to suggest that the structure of the brain is susceptible to environmental experience. He concludes that 'brain specialization and anatomy can be influenced by culture' (p. 78)—a functionalist's implicit rejection of Moro's assertion that the brain determines language. It is salient that neither Moro nor Everett adverts to the research that the other party brings to light.

1.5 On the Architecture of Formalism
Versus Functionalism

It is worth noting from the outset that modern formalism is strongly centripetal, if not isomorphic, while modern functionalism is much more internally diverse, so that no single example can stand for the whole. Our initial case study foreshadows this characteristic difference in the internal structure of the two approaches, a matter to which Chapters 3 and 4 will return. Contemporary generative grammar, Moro's foundation, is the dominant present-day version of formalism. Although Moro doesn't represent the whole of formalism, he writes from inside its modern center. In contrast, Everett writes from the edge of one of several varieties of functionalism. His insistence that language is a cultural tool seems to presuppose, rather than directly assert, that 'form follows function' in the sense that what language is a tool for is culturally embedded communication.

In commentary on his 2012 book that addresses this point, Everett labeled his style of linguistics as compatible with functionalism but distinct from it (2013: 647). Consulting the composite characterization of functionalism in the Appendix shows that Everett's assumptions and working habits are strongly functionalist: inductive; restrained in the search for generalizations; attentive to speakers' performance rather than their internal states and to language differences across sub-groups of speakers. Moro, the linguist-engineer, and Everett, the linguist-collector, do not hold comparable positions within their respective formalist versus functionalist domains, nor do those domains have commensurable internal architecture. Still, we can start from here.

References

Chomsky, Noam. (1980). *Rules and representations*. New York: Columbia University Press.

Chomsky, Noam. (1995). *The Minimalist Program*. Cambridge, MA: MIT Press.

Curnow, Timothy J. (2002). [Review of the book *Functionalism and formalism in linguistics*]. *Studies in Language* 26(2): 505–512.

Enfield, N. J. (2013). 'What I'm reading: Language, culture, and mind: Trends and standards in the latest pendulum swing' [Review of the book *Language: The cultural tool*]. *Journal of the Royal Anthropological Institute* 19: 155–169.

Everett, Daniel L. (2008) *Don't sleep, there are snakes: Life and language in the Amazonian jungle*. New York: Pantheon.

Everett, Daniel L. (2012). *Language: The cultural tool*. New York: Random House.

Everett, Daniel L. (2013). 'The state of whose art? Reply to Nick Enfield's review of *Language: The cultural tool*'. *Journal of the Royal Anthropological Institute* 19: 645–648.

Fischer, Olga. (2007). *Morphosyntactic change: Functional and formal perspectives*. Oxford: Oxford University Press.

McWhorter, John. (2012, 8 April). 'Repeat after me' [Review of the book *Language: The Cultural Tool*]. *The New York Times* (p. BR16). Retrieved from www.nytimes.com/2012/04/08/books/review/language-the-cultural-tool-by-daniel-l-everett.html

Moro, Andrea. (2016). *Impossible languages*. Cambridge, MA: MIT Press.

Radford, Tim. (2012, 15 March). [Review of the book *Language: The cultural tool*]. *The Guardian*. Retrieved from www.theguardian.com/books/2012/mar/15/language-cultural-daniel-everett-review

Sullivan, Louis H. (1896). 'The tall office building artistically considered'. *Lippincott's Magazine* 57(3): 406.

Tomlinson, Antony. (2012, September/October). [Review of the book *Language: The cultural tool*]. *Philosophy Now* 92(2). Retrieved from https://philosophynow.org/issues/92/Language_The_Cultural_Tool_by_Daniel_Everett.

Williams, R. (2012, 2 May). 'Review of Daniel Everett's new book *Language: The Cultural Tool*' [web log comment]. Retrieved from https://philosophyandpsychology.wordpress.com/2012/05/02/review-of-daniel-everetts-new-book-language-the-cultural-tool/

2 Background to the Current Debate

2.1 Is There a Starting Point?

Recalling that the lists in the Appendix characterize, rather than define, formalist versus functionalist linguistics, one might ask whether this juxtaposition of traits still makes sense when we look at linguistics before the present day. That is to say, is it only in contemporary study of language that we can offset, say, formalists' embrace of abstraction; the priority they place on theory construction; or their engineer-like attention to the inner framework of language, to functionalists' efforts to coordinate language forms and functions; their collector-like scrutiny of particulars and specific cases; and their restraint in matters of theory? To what extent did earlier study of language associate subsets of these traits into two internally coherent approaches, dissociated externally to face each other? Or, is it even possible to discern what preceded modern formalism and functionalism in these terms?

Remarkably, there has been little reflection on whether the confrontation between formalism and functionalism has much of a past. If we take the *terminus a quo* to be self-conscious recognition that an approach to language labeled with the term 'formalist' stands in opposition to another labeled 'functionalist', then tension between the two may only go back to the 1960s or 1970s (Graffi 2001: 389; Carnie & Mendoza-Denton 2003: 375). However, this account of the debate casts functionalism as a counterpoint to the emergence in the United States of Noam Chomsky's distinctively formalist generative theory. That account truncates the history of both formalism and functionalism. The coinage of these terms as a pair of opposites—with their rewarding alliteration and near-matched metrical structure—may be a product of the late twentieth century, but the ideas about language that they label preceded them.

A partial exception to the tendency to neglect the historical backdrop goes a little further back in time to identify an antecedent to functionalism in the 1930s work of the Prague Linguistic Circle, to be discussed below. For example, Newmeyer's (1998; 2001) exposition of formalism versus functionalism adverts to Prague Circle linguistics. On the formalist side, however, Newmeyer grounds the debate in the emergence of generative grammar (1998: 7–9), obviating the question of whether there was any pre-generativist, but still formalist, style of language study that acted as a principled alternative to functionalism before the middle of the twentieth century. With the exception of an aside in Battistella (2000: 431), reviews of Newmeyer's book seem to take his stance for granted, and comment on his theme of conflict between formalism and functionalism as if it had no relevant antecedents (e.g., Carstairs-McCarthy 1999; Haspelmath 2000; Morvacsik 2000; Tallerman 2000; Foolen 2002; Francis 2002).

In narrowly modern terms, formalism studies language as a formal object without reference to its role in communication, while functionalism insists that communication imposes such an essential shape on language that it cannot be studied meaningfully without reference to its function. In this text, I identify formalism and functionalism in terms that are somewhat broader than those that have currency right now; by those lights, both points of view have precedents long before the 1960s or 1970s. It goes beyond the ambitions of this text to narrate the full, multi-dimensional story of the development of formalism and of functionalism, assuming that that is even achievable. Still, identifying some of the ancestors to formalism and functionalism illuminates the scope of the controversy between the two. Chapter 2 first sketches some pre-twentieth-century ideas about the nature of language that serve as the distant backdrop to the modern debate. After that, we turn to identifiably formalist linguistics from 1900 up to the late middle of the twentieth century, then likewise for functionalist linguistics.

2.2 Before the Twentieth Century

It is worth noting that those few publications which swim against the tide to take a longer-term view of the history of the debate (e.g., Bates & MacWhinney 1982; Dirven & Fried 1987; Croft 1993; Givón 2013) are the work of functionalists rather than formalists. Functionalists seem more willing than formalists to inquire into their own forerunners and more open to viewing their work as part of a stream of research, as opposed to emphasizing the novelty of their ideas about language.

By the light of this fact, it is striking that one of the very earliest studies of language cited as part of the general background to western language science has a distinctively formalist cast: the Sanskrit scholar Pāṇini's *Aṣṭādhyāyī*, created around 500 BCE in what is now Pakistan (Katre 1987; Cardona 1988). The *Aṣṭādhyāyī* is an arch-economical exposition of the grammar of Sanskrit, written in the form of about 4,000 pithy ordered statements, or *sūtra*s, which distill the complex facts of Sanskrit morphophonetics and morphosyntax. Pāṇinian *sūtra*s, designed to be memorized, communicate the grammar of Sanskrit in a uniquely parsimonious style which pares away any intrusion of redundancy or ambiguity. Separate from the *Aṣṭādhyāyī* but traditionally also attributed to Pāṇini are three ancillary texts: an ordered inventory of the sounds of the language; a catalogue of verbal roots; and a list of nominal stems and other lexical items to which the *sūtra*s refer. The goal of the *Aṣṭādhyāyī* is to specify the forms of the language through the operation of interacting layers of rules and metarules. The system acts on roots to produce abstract intermediate forms which are modified, step by step, into the recognizable words of Sanskrit while non-occurring forms are eliminated. Pāṇini's grammar also accounts for certain facets of dialectal variation but without losing its focus on form or expostulating on topics such as the scope of language variation or the significance of a speaker's choice of one speech style over another. Throughout, the *Aṣṭādhyāyī* models a commitment to the systematicity of grammar as a set of formal operations that are fully tractable to analysis.

Indian scholarship has highly valued the depth and intricacy of Pāṇini's *Aṣṭādhyāyī* and responded to it with centuries of commentary and exegesis, much of which has itself been the basis of further commentary and analysis. When Europeans discovered the text and its commentarial tradition in the late 1700s, it gave westerners access to the grammar of Sanskrit and demonstrated some of the remarkable patterned complexities of the language. Eventually, the great finesse and sophistication of Pāṇini's work dawned on scholars from Europe (Staal 1972). Once they recognized the historical relationship of Sanskrit to Latin and Greek, analysis of Sanskrit became a cornerstone in the reconstruction of the Indo-European language family, the major preoccupation of the study of language in Europe from the late 1700s through the 1800s (Morpurgo Davies 1998).

Among later-generation students of Pāṇini's grammar was the leading American formalist Leonard Bloomfield (1887–1949), a long-time admirer of the *Aṣṭādhyāyī* (Bloomfield 1927, 1929). Bloomfield held in high esteem Pāṇini's descriptivism, his concise style, and his goal of comprehensive and rigorous analysis of every form of the language. Bloomfield self-consciously emulated Pāṇini in his work on the Algonquian language Menomini and in his classic 1933 text *Language* (Emeneau 1988). Most importantly for our concerns here, Bloomfield's *Menomini Morphophonemics* (1939) embraced Pāṇini's adoption of abstract forms and his reduction of the complexities of a natural grammar to the output of a set of ordered operations—both hallmarks of formalism. The formalist complexion of the *Aṣṭādhyāyī* is enhanced by its separation of the rules governing morphophonology and morphosyntax from lists of roots and sounds, a move that seems to foreshadow the notion of modularity in the organization of a grammar. Among Pāṇini's contemporary admirers is Noam Chomsky, who identifies the *Aṣṭādhyāyī* as a generative grammar (Chomsky 1965: v; Dillinger &

Palácio 1997). Unlike Bloomfield, who acknowledged modeling his work on Pāṇini's grammar, Chomsky does not claim a direct line of descent from Pāṇini to generative grammar. Rather, Chomsky views generative grammar as an independent innovation that shares some surprising common ground with ancient Indian grammatical analysis.

In these ways, Pāṇini's work prefigured some traits of modern formalism. Among other ancient-world scholars who contributed to the study of language, Plato (fourth century BCE) and Aristotle (384–322 BCE) are prominent, although neither wrote a full-scale grammar. Granted the breadth and complexity of both philosophers' ideas and their pervasive impacts on western culture, it is not obvious how to map them onto either formalism or functionalism—or even whether that mapping is fruitful. Nevertheless, one can't miss that in the writings of modern formalists the name of ('idealist') Plato is much more likely to surface than that of Aristotle (who famously observed and collected all manner of natural phenomena)—and vice versa among functionalists. For example, Chomsky (1986) popularized the expression 'Plato's problem' with reference to a passage in Plato's dialogue *Meno* in which Socrates elicits the principles of geometry from an uneducated slave boy. Chomsky's point is that child language learners can be shown to have surprising depth of understanding of grammar which is neither taught nor demonstrated to them: like Plato's slave boy, they know more than can be readily accounted for on the basis of their outward experience. On the opposite side, the prominent 'west coast functionalist' Talmy Givón (b. 1936) routinely cites Aristotle's articulation of the core notion of functionalism in biology, namely, that the forms of living beings match their functions, so that, for example, birds that live in swampy areas have long legs and webbed feet, while those that consume nuts have short, sturdy beaks. For Givón, the best point of departure for functionalism resides in biology, a discipline into which Aristotle infused a functionalist perspective over two thousand years ago (2002: 1–7, 2013). In these ways, both Chomsky and Givón find warrants for certain facets of their views about language by looking backward to ancient Greek scholarship.

In addition, Plato's most extensive treatment of language matters, his famous dialogue *Cratylus*, centers on an issue that divides modern formalists from functionalists. *Cratylus* is a meditation on the question of whether the shapes and sounds of words are intrinsic to their meanings, or whether the association of words to meanings is merely conventional (Joseph 2000). It is framed as a conversation between Socrates and two collegial adversaries who hold opposite positions on the nature of words and meanings. One is the conventionalist Hermogenes, who asserts that words are connected to meanings arbitrarily by human habit or custom. The other is Cratylus, who argues that the relationship of words to meanings has natural force, with sounds intimately connected to meanings. Plato's dialogue works these ideas out in the cultural and intellectual terms of ancient Greece, many of which are understandably alien to modern language scholarship. Overlooking the centuries that separate Plato's day from ours, there is an echo of *Cratylus* in modern formalists' presupposition that words and forms are arbitrarily connected to their meanings, as opposed to functionalists' commitment to iconicity as an important force in phonology, word-formation, and grammar. On most readings, Plato does not settle the issue in *Cratylus*. Contemporary debate about iconicity does not invoke Plato's authority, but it is salient that this facet of what divides modern formalists and functionalists has such a long history.

Much more could be written about the development, between the third or fourth century BCE and the beginning of the twentieth century, of the ideas about language relevant to modern formalism and functionalism. One landmark might be Chomsky's historiographical research centering on Cartesian linguistics (1966), a potential counter-example to formalist disinclination toward the history of linguistics. However, Chomsky's concern in this problematic text is with Cartesian rationalism, which he contends shares some of the characteristics of generative theory (Thomas 2009). Whether or not Chomsky's reading of seventeenth-century texts is persuasive, rationalism is not inherent to formalism, so that *Cartesian Linguistics* makes little contribution to identifying the ancestors of formalism. Moreover, Chomsky is virtually alone among generativists in his interest in historical matters. Modern generativists sometimes cite Chomsky's historiography, but few either address the critical response to it or independently probe earlier versions of formalism.

Taking up the thread again at the beginning of the 1900s, the Swiss linguist Ferdinand de Saussure (1857–1913) is conventionally identified as a turning-point between nineteenth-century historical-comparative linguistics and modern structuralist linguistics, which conceives of language as a complex relationship of systems. In this sense, Saussurean structuralism pervades all modern linguistics up to the present day. However, the central exposition of Saussure's linguistics, the posthumously published *Course in General Linguistics* (1916 / 1983, the '*Cours*') as assembled by his students, presents formidable hermeneutic challenges, so that it is not clear how his ideas have affected the debate between formalists and functionalists. Dirven and Fried (1987: xi) imply that Saussure's influence is felt more broadly among functionalists but deny that he can be identified with either side. Joseph (2002) has studied how Bloomfield and Chomsky (two formalists already part of our narrative) each positioned themselves relative to Saussure's linguistics. In both cases, Joseph finds a complex record of selective readings and mis-readings of the *Cours* and shifts in positions over time. Among functionalists, Givón (1995) stakes out a strong anti-Saussurean position. He considers three of Saussure's trademark contributions to have strengthened formalism at the expense of functionalism: the Saussurean doctrine of arbitrariness 'detached the linguistic sign—the visible behavior—

from its invisible mental correlates'; Saussure's distinction between *langue* and *parole* idealizes away the rich, indeterminant, and essential parts of language; and Saussure's segregation of diachrony from synchrony similarly dismisses the complexities of variation and change which functionalists find valuable (1995: 5–7). Not all functionalists would agree with Givón, nor do all formalists accept the full scope of Saussure's ideas. Nevertheless, those ideas have helped each group define its own commitments.

2.3 Twentieth-Century Formalist Linguistics to 1950

Dirven and Fried (1987: xi) present an intriguing graphic display summarizing their view of the separate descents of formalism and functionalism from 1900. On the functionalist side, they link Saussure by lines of influence to multiple schools of European structuralism: Geneva, Prague, London, and the Netherlands, each of which heads a list of adherents. (Note that with this, Dirven and Fried counter Givón's reading, which puts Saussure at odds with functionalism.) The formalist side is comparatively underpopulated, with Saussure's influence extending to a single school, that in Copenhagen. An independent line of descent of formalism runs parallel, but is unlinked to Saussure, labeled 'Descriptivism'. Under this heading the American anthropologist Franz Boas first subsumes 'Bloomfield etc.'. Chomsky's generative grammar follows under Bloomfield, with 'Cognitivism', identified with George Lakoff and Ronald Langacker, conceived as a second generation below Boas. Kenneth Pike is entered off to the side, as a non-Boasian formalist.

Dirven and Fried's diagram could be criticized from several angles. Many would dispute the classification of Lakoff, Langacker, and Pike as formalists; Chomsky would reject the implication that his work descends from that of Bloomfield; and the absence of any role for Boas's prominent student Edward Sapir is conspicuous. But putting these reservations aside, Dirven and Fried's attribution of twentieth-century formalism to American scholars is striking, as is the priority they give to Boas.

Franz Boas (1858–1942) was trained in physics and geography, then left Germany for what is now the Canadian territory of Nunavut in 1883 to research the cultural effects of extreme cold weather. On site, he was captivated by the culture and languages of the Inuit people. Despite having no formal training in linguistics, Boas eventually made a career out of studying Native American languages, especially those of the Pacific Northwest. He developed a working style that proved very influential: in direct face-to-face interactions with a speaker, Boas elicited and transcribed oral narratives, then translated them word-by-word. The output of his method was a description of the grammar of the target language arrived at by close scrutiny of the transcribed corpus without relying on the features or analytic categories of any other language.

Boas is now considered one of the founders of American anthropological linguistics. Both his methods and his focus on the study of Native American languages had lasting impact. Boasian insistence on inferring a grammar from the output of a speaker, meticulously recorded and analyzed, provided one of the building blocks of what became American structuralist linguistics. The term 'structuralism' is a fraught one (Hymes & Fought 1981). Even restricting its use to the context of the study of the language in the United States, it cannot be identified in any facile way with the term 'formalism'. Nevertheless, American structuralist linguistics has a formalist orientation. Some of that character is registered in Boasian empiricism, but Boas also reflected at length on language, culture, and thought (1911), so that Hymes (1961: 90) characterizes Boas as 'clearing the way for, but not quite occupying the ground of, his structurally-minded successors'.

Among Boas's most prominent successors was Leonard Bloomfield. Bloomfield was never a direct student of Boas, but he inherited Boasian methods and brought them together with other intellectual forces to create a distinctive and highly influential style of linguistics. One of those forces was his admiration for Pāṇini; another was his drive to establish an autonomous discipline of linguistics in the United States that was recognizably a science of language. With the prestige of science ascendant, Bloomfield assumed both institutional leadership as a founder of the Linguistic Society of America, and intellectual leadership in striving to replace philosophical speculation about language, mind, and culture with an emphasis on attested facts. In early mid-career, Bloomfield adopted behaviorism, a school of psychology in which, applied to language, the goal was to eliminate unobservable 'mentalistic' concepts like 'mind', 'memory', 'thought'. He favored the terms 'mechanistic' for his preferred style of analysis, and 'descriptivism' for his approach overall. In this way, Bloomfield prioritized observable forms, and called attention to his principled reticence to approach language from the point of view of its role in communication.

A short 1926 article published in *Language*, 'A Set of Postulates for the Science of Language', illustrates Bloomfield's formalism. On the model of mathematics, he attempted to specify a set of axioms—definitions of terms and assumptions following from those definitions—on which basis a linguistics independent of anthropology, acoustics, physiology, and (in particular) psychology could be built. Bloomfield's postulates concentrate on defining the forms of language and the characteristics of those forms, with meaning conceived of as a 'recurrent stimulus-reaction which corresponds to a form' (p. 155). Contrary to his reputation, Bloomfield did not reject analyses that took recourse to meaning, either the meaning of words or the meanings of constructions. Rather, he considered semantics an underdeveloped subfield, so that (in his view) the scientific basis of linguistics should start with the material forms of language, rather than what those forms communicated. He wrote: 'linguists, confronted with the parallelism of form and meaning,

choose form as the basis for classification' (1926: 157). With this, Bloomfield implicitly rejected the functionalist maxim 'form follows function'.

Bloomfieldian formalism and Bloomfield's drive to create a science
of language had a major impact on linguistics in early twentieth-century
America. A group of his students and followers that goes by the name of
the 'post-Bloomfieldians' developed a distinctive body of formalist work
that carried forward some, but not all, of his ideas. Although they inherited
Bloomfield's conception of linguistics as a science of language, they did
not adopt behaviorism. The post-Bloomfieldians extended the prioritization
of form over meaning beyond Bloomfield's reticence with semantics, to
develop a style of linguistic analysis that some called 'distributionalism'.
Distributionalism attempted on principled grounds to describe linguistic
structure solely with reference to the co-occurrence of linguistic units. For
example, a distributionalist would declare that, in English, /p/ and /b/ represent independent phonemes not because a *pen* is where farm animals live
and *Ben* is a man's name, but rather because initial /p/ is aspirated and /b/
is not aspirated, and because the sequence /mp/ appears as a syllabic coda,
whereas /mb/ does not.

A theoretical innovation of one of the post-Bloomfieldians demonstrates
their formalist orientation. A paper by Charles Hockett (1954) explored
what he called 'two models of grammatical description': 'item-and-process'
versus 'item-and-arrangement'. In the former, two linguistic units might be
compared as outputs of differing processes that operate on the same root,
such as suffixation of the word *chat* to yield *chatting*, versus reduplication
to yield *chitchat*. In contrast, an 'item-and-arrangement' approach would
compare the two units without presupposing that they are derived from the
same root: in one unit, a free form (*chat[t]*) precedes a bound morpheme
(*-ing*); in the other unit, two near-identical free forms (*chit; chat*) occur
adjacent to each other. Hockett even-handedly assessed the strengths and
weaknesses in both approaches, even as he found item-and-arrangement
more tractable because he considered it to have been more thoroughly
formalized—and to Hockett, formalization of a theoretical tool was a top
priority.

Another post-Bloomfieldian innovation illustrates how far some distributionalists pushed their style of formalism. 'Immediate Constituent Analysis'
was an analytic technique they developed to display the internal structure
of words and groups of words as nested, hierarchically organized constituents. In Hockett's example (1958: 152), the string *a man are* (in *The sons
and daughters of a man are his children*) would not form an immediate
constituent on the basis of the observation that alone it constituted only
'a meaningless sequence of morphemes'. In contrast, Gleason (1961: 132)
distrusted reliance on 'uncontrolled intuition' which he felt was implied in
this way of defining constituent boundaries. Gleason proposed alternative

criteria for establishing constituent boundaries, based on substitutability (*a man* is a constituent because it can be substituted by *he*, whereas there is no obvious substitute for *a man are*) or freedom of occurrence (the utterance *a man* can stand alone, but not so *a man are*). Gleason's version of Immediate Constituent Analysis comes closer to the spirit of distributionalism, but both Gleason and Hockett take formalist approaches, designed to meet a formalist goal, namely the identification and organization of units and sub-units of language. Notice, for instance, how devoid these techniques of analysis are of reference to speakers' communicative intentions. In Chapter 3 we will return to the development of the legacies of Bloomfield and the post-Bloomfieldians, to bring out both continuity and innovation in twenty-first century formalism.

2.4 Twentieth-Century Functionalism from the Prague Circle to Pike

While the study of language evolved in the United States to meet the specifically formalist goals of early twentieth-century American science of language, in Europe functionalism flourished. Locally based scholars in Geneva, Prague, London, and the Netherlands emerged and developed their own working styles. Saussure's *Cours* was a major stimulus, although each group defined its own position relative to Saussurean doctrines, and relative to the powerful model of Prague Circle functionalism.

It is worthwhile keeping in mind from the start that some participants in early twentieth-century linguistics in Europe and the U.S. disrupt this general scenario. In Denmark, for example, the Linguistic Circle of Copenhagen was founded on the direct inspiration of the functionalist-oriented Prague Linguistic Circle. However, the central figure of the Copenhagen circle, Louis Hjelmslev (1899–1965), developed a grammatical theory on the model of mathematics, which he called 'glossematics'. The goal of glossematics was to deduce from formal statements an inventory of categories for the analysis, at a rigorously high level of abstraction, of both sounds and forms in any language. Hjelmslev's austere formalism stands out; however, he also developed a sophisticated semiotics that went beyond Saussure's notions of signifier versus signified to analyze the relationships of expression, content, form, and substance. In this facet of his work, Hjelmslev was a major influence on the twentieth-century functionalist Michael Halliday, discussed in Chapter 4.

An older compatriot of Hjelmslev, the Danish grammarian and historical linguist Otto Jespersen (1860–1943), likewise cannot easily be identified with either side of the formalist/functionalist divide. Jespersen distanced himself from Saussure and did not ally himself with any of the post-Saussurean schools, regardless of their formalist or functionalist tendencies. Instead,

Jespersen produced a wealth of sensitive, innovative writings on phonetics, the history and structure of English, language teaching—which moved deftly from form to function and vice versa. Jespersen also insisted that language scholarship be rooted in the record of real language data, as used by real people, to communicate real messages. Both Hjelmslev and Jespersen contributed to the linguistics of the day from outside its general trends. Moreover, although a formalist mindset dominated mainstream American linguistics in the relevant period, there were figures (discussed below) whose work does not fit this profile.

With that caveat in place, what follows is a sketch of how functionalist ideas infused language scholarship in Europe in the first half of the twentieth century (Toman 1995; Akamatsu 2001). Under most accounts, a significant event was the foundation of the Prague Linguistic Circle in 1926, which began as a series of meetings for informal discussion among three linguists, the Czech Vilém Mathesius (1882–1945) and Russian émigrés Nikolaj Trubetzkoy (1890–1938) and Roman Jakobson (1886–1982). The three shared a dissatisfaction with the Neogrammarian historical-comparativists in Leipzig, who asserted the mechanical exceptionlessness of sound laws. They also shared an attraction to Saussure's claim that languages can be studied as coherent systems at any point in time. From the start, in the text of their 'Ten Theses' published in 1929 as the group's manifesto, the Prague scholars boldly announced their functionalist orientation: 'language is a system of means of expression adapted to a goal' (Vachek 1967: 33). Jakobson (1965), for example, collected examples of how language form adapts to its function: *Veni, vidi, vici* communicates not only Caesar's deeds, but the order in which he accomplished them; in *high, higher, highest* the three-stage incremental increase in word length iconically signals incremental increase in height; a shared rhyme in the words *bash, smash, clash, splash*, etc., represents a shared semantic feature (perhaps, 'loss of control'). For members of the Prague Circle, units at various levels of organization of a language served the purposes of communication: communication of meaning; of the speaker's identity or emotional state; of an effect the speaker wishes to induce in the listener. The Prague Circle enthusiastically engaged in research on many language phenomena, including literature, especially poetry; language change; language standardization and planning; language typology; language and culture. Here we will examine two of their most consequential and best-developed topics, with the clearest ties to modern functionalism: phonology and syntax.

The Prague Circle separated phonology from phonetics on functional grounds: phonetics studies the substance and production of sounds, but since phonetic units do not communicate meaning, phonetics lies outside the center of linguistics proper. Phonology, on the other hand, is a core subfield of linguistics, because sounds map onto functions: unlike for the American distributionalists, for the Prague Circle, English /p/ and /b/ represent distinctive phonemes because a *pen* is where farm animals live and *Ben* is a man's name. The first job of the linguist is not to record a language's inventory of sounds, but to locate what counts as a phonological opposition: the functional difference between *pen* and *Ben* signals that voicing of initial stop consonants is a significant phonological opposition in English.

From the early 1900s many scholars had been working out various notions of what became the concept of the 'phoneme': some abstract, some material, some psychological, some as more or less discrete units. Among Prague Circle members, Jakobson's and Trubetzkoy's conceptions of the phoneme did not wholly converge. But as a minimum the two agreed that phonemes comprised bundles of phonic properties later called 'distinctive features'. The notion of 'archiphoneme'—a label for a phonological unit that neutralizes the difference between two distinctive phonemes that appear in specific positions—briefly flourished in Prague Circle writings. Archiphonemes and distinctive features signal the Prague Circle's openness to abstract analyses and their interest in locating language universals, two traits more typical of formalists than functionalists. Nevertheless, their basic methodological commitment to locating differences in form via differences in meaning grounds the essentially functionalist character of their work.

In syntax, the functionalism of the Prague Circle is very fully displayed. The group developed a 'Functional Sentence Perspective' (FSP) as a principled means to bring their ideas to bear on word order and other syntactic facts cross-linguistically. The FSP divides sentence constituents into 'theme' (old information; information previously registered in the discourse) and 'rheme' (new, unpredictable information; information that drives the discourse forward), and then analyzes the position of thematic versus rhematic elements. For example, the sentence 'Shakespeare wrote *Othello*' positions '*Othello*' in the sentence-final rhematic ('new information') position; it is likely the answer to the question 'What did Shakespeare write?' In contrast, the sentence '*Othello* was written by Shakespeare' treats '*Othello*' as the theme ('old information') and 'Shakespeare' as the rheme; it is likely the answer to the question 'Who wrote *Othello*?' In this example, what the FSP addresses is how communicative function maps onto the syntax of English subjects and objects. The FSP goes beyond word order to examine other factors that bear on information structure, including intonation and word choice (e.g., the differing argument structures of the verbs in *I like cold weather* versus *Cold weather suits me*). A latter-day Prague scholar, Jan Firbas (1921–2000) contributed the notion of 'communicative dynamism', which admits that linguistic units exhibit relative degrees of communicative dynamism rather than an all-or-nothing identification as theme (less communicatively dynamic) versus rheme (highly dynamic).

As an aside, if one were to apply the Prague Circle's FSP to Louis Sullivan's famous saying, 'form follows function', a buried linguistic irony emerges. In the expression itself the word 'form' *precedes*, not follows, the word 'function' so that the structure of this aphorism actually contradicts its meaning. Insofar as functionalists have reflected on this twist, they may simply savor its incongruity. Alternatively, they might notice that in 'form follows function' what counts as presupposed, thematic, material with reduced communicative dynamism—the word 'form'—appears earlier in the expression, while the more salient, more communicatively dynamic element—'function'—appears in final, rhematic, position.

World War II interrupted the careers, and in some cases destroyed the lives, of many participants in early twentieth-century European functionalism. Some fled Europe for the United States. Among them was Roman Jakobson, who brought his brand of Prague Circle functionalism to New York and later to Harvard and MIT. Although Jakobson became an internationally known figure, Prague Circle linguistics played a more limited role in the history of functionalism in the United States, with its influence falling mostly on one subgroup, what Newmeyer (2001) calls 'formal functionalists' (see Chapter 4).

Another scholar who emigrated to New York during the war, André Martinet (1908–1999), later returned to Paris to build up an important strand of functionalist linguistics. His work was based on a not uncritical reading of Saussure, which integrated some touches of both Praguean and even Hjelmslevian linguistics. A key principle of Martinet's functionalism is that of 'relevance' (sometimes 'communicative relevance'), by which he aims to pinpoint meaning-bearing elements of language. For example, Martinet points out that order is highly relevant at the level of phonemes: the words *clay*, *lake*, and *kale* comprise the same three phonemes, but instantiated in three different orders, whereas in syntax he asserts that 'the relevancy of order is far from general: it is fairly immaterial whether I say *the one I like is Paul* or *Paul is the one I like*' (1962: 41)—a claim some functionalists might dispute. Martinet brought his functionalism to bear on the sound patterns of language in extensive discussion of phonetics and phonetic change, intonation, pitch, tone, and syllable structure, but also addressed topics in morphosyntax, language typology, diachronic linguistics, and dialectology. The notion of 'relevance' shares with the Prague School term 'communicative dynamism' an intuitive appeal, a certain vagueness of definition—and a clear functionalist orientation.

Although Martinet's functionalism is well-established in Europe, especially in France, it had less impact on American linguistics. However, at least two other important figures in early-to-mid-twentieth-century American linguistics are recognizably functionalist. The first was one of Boas's most prominent students, Edward Sapir (1884–1939). Sapir began his career following Boas's footsteps, carrying out linguistic-ethnographic fieldwork in the Pacific Northwest. His work shows unusually keen powers of observation and analysis. Later, as a faculty member at the University of Pennsylvania, Sapir worked with Tony Tillohash, a young speaker of Southern Paiute whom the Bureau of Indian Affairs had displaced from his home in Utah to attend the Carlisle Indian School in Carlisle, Pennsylvania. Working with Tillohash, Sapir developed his conception of the psychological reality of the phoneme. He found that Tillohash perceived the sounds of Southern Paiute as distinctive not with reference to their perceptible acoustic properties, but rather with reference to his feeling for their roles in the sound system of the language. That is to say, Tillohash prioritized the function of a sound over its structural properties. Sapir's work overall was unabashedly functionalist in that he viewed language as a psychologically embedded cultural practice, which shapes speakers' experience:

> Language is at one and the same time helping and retarding us in our exploration of experience, and the details of these processes of help and hindrance are deposited in the subtler meanings of different cultures. [...] It is this constant interplay between language and experience which removes language from the cold status of such purely and simply symbolic systems as mathematical symbolism of flag signaling. [. . .] language may not only refer to experience or even mold, interpret, and discover experience, but [. . .] it also substitutes for it.
>
> (Sapir 1933 / 1949: 11)

Sapir and Bloomfield were near-contemporaries, although Sapir's humanism contrasts strongly with Bloomfield's behaviorism and pursuit of formalist rigor. Bloomfield had greater effect on the institutionalization of mid-century American structuralist linguistics, but Sapir inspired many functionalist-oriented linguists, and continues to be cited respectfully by contemporary functionalists (e.g., Givón 1995: 1; Halliday 1999; Van Valin 2007).

A generation after Bloomfield and Sapir, another American linguist, Kenneth Pike (1912–2000) worked out an original grammatical theory with a functionalist character. Pike was associated throughout his long career with the Christian evangelical organization now known as SIL International, which trains missionaries in linguistic fieldwork and Bible translation. Pike served as a missionary-linguist studying Mixtec in Mexico in the early 1930s before entering a doctoral program at the University of Michigan. He eventually became a faculty member there while continuing as an active fieldworker and trainer of missionary-linguists. Pike developed an ambitious, synthetic grammatical theory, 'tagmemics'. The word was coined (by Bloomfield but developed by Pike) on the model of 'phonemics' to label the minimal grammatical element. Tagmemics analyzed how 'fillers' correlated with syntactic 'slots' as, for example, the fillers *my roommate* or *Klara* may fill the same slot in *[ ] applied to law school*. A sequence of tagmemes makes up a 'syntagmeme', and so on up to higher and higher levels of organization. For Pike, those higher and higher levels extended seamlessly from sentences to paragraphs to discourse to gesture to nonverbal behavior to all manner of cultural practices. Because for Pike language was a non-autonomous resource within general human communicative practice, the analytic categories and tools of linguistics could apply across the board: Pike (1954–1960 / 1967) famously ends with an analysis in the spirit of tagmemics of a football game.

Pike's work orbited far from the formalism of his contemporaries, in several ways. It was explicitly designed to help fieldworkers make sense of a foreign-language corpus, in their preparation for Bible translation. Pike did not participate in the distributionalists' reluctance to use meaning as an analytic tool or to rely on speakers' intuitions. Most of all, Pike's integration of language with culture made tagmemics distinctively functionalist. It is notable that Dan Everett, author of *Language, the Cultural Tool,* first met the Pirahã people as a member of SIL International, the institution that Pike led.

2.5 Why the Background Matters

The goal of Chapter 2 has been to point out some of the precursors to modern formalism and functionalism. Early twenty-first century formalist linguistics has unique features, as does early twenty-first century functionalism. Still, many of the fieldmarks that differentiate the two approaches are recognizable as far back in the history of the study of language as the eye can see. Pāṇini aimed to build a comprehensive grammar; the engineer in him produced a penetrating, concise, self-contained model of Sanskrit. In *Cratylus*, Plato gave to Cratylus the role of champion of the notion that words mirror the essential nature of their referents, an idea that Saussure challenged but that Jakobson would adopt and remodel in hoisting a functionalist flag over his evidence that iconicity shapes grammar, word-forms, and sound patterns. In the early twentieth-century, post-Bloomfieldian linguist-engineers dominated in the United States, while linguist-collectors amassed evidence for how the Prague Circle's communicative dynamism, Martinet's 'relevance', and Sapir's and Pike's different commitments to the integration of language and culture made the study of language (in their eyes) broader, richer, and more powerful. None of this earlier work precisely foreshadows how formalism and functionalism developed after the 1950s, but the existence of that work prepares us to better understand how more recent work arose, and to notice what is novel in it.

References

Akamatsu, Tsutomu. (2001). 'The development of functionalism from the Prague School to the present'. In Sylvain Auroux, E. F. K. Koerner, Hans-Josef Niederehe, and Kees Versteegh (Eds.), *History of the language sciences*, vol. 2 (pp. 1768–1789). Berlin: Walter de Gruyter.

Bates, Elizabeth and Brian MacWhinney. (1982). 'Functionalist approaches to grammar'. In Eric Wanner and Lila R. Gleitman (Eds.), *Language acquisition: The state of the art* (pp. 173–218). Cambridge: Cambridge University Press.

Battistella, Edwin. (2000). [Review of the book *Language form and language function*]. *Journal of Linguistics* 36: 431–439.

Bloomfield, Leonard. (1926). 'A set of postulates for the science of language'. *Language* 2: 153–164.

Bloomfield, Leonard. (1927). 'On Some Rules of Pāṇini'. *Journal of the American Oriental Society* 47: 61–70. doi: 10.2307/593241.

Bloomfield, Leonard. (1929). [Review of the book *Konkordanz Pāṇini-Candra*]. *Language* 5(4): 267–276. doi: 10.2307/409597.

Bloomfield, Leonard. (1933). *Language*. New York: Henry Holt.

Bloomfield, Leonard. (1939). 'Menomini morphophonemics'. *Travaux du cercle linguistique de Prague* 8: 105–115.

Boas, Franz. (1911). 'Introduction'. In *Handbook of American Indian Languages* (pp. 1–83). Washington DC: Bureau of American Ethnology.

Cardona, George. (1988) *Pāṇini: His work and its tradition: Vol. 1. Background and introduction*. Delhi: Motilal Banarsidass.

Carnie, Andrew and Norma Mendoza-Denton. (2003). 'Functionalism is/n't formalism: An interactive review of Darnell et al. (1999)'. *Journal of Linguistics* 39: 373–389.

Carstairs-McCarthy, Andrew. (1999). [Review of the book *Language form and language function*]. *Anthropological Linguistics* 41: 426–429.

Chomsky, Noam. (1965). *Aspects of the theory of syntax*. Cambridge, MA: MIT Press.

Chomsky, Noam. (1966). *Cartesian linguistics: A chapter in the history of rationalist thought*. New York: Harper and Row.

Chomsky, Noam. (1986). *Knowledge of language*. New York: Praeger.

Croft, William. (1993). 'Functional-typological theory in its historical and intellectual context'. *Sprachtypologie und Universalienforschung (STUF)* 46(1/4): 15–26.

Dillinger, Mike and Adair Palácio. (1997). 'Generative linguistics: Development and perspectives. An interview with Noam Chomsky'. *Chomsky no Brasil/Chomsky in Brazil*. Special edition of *Revista de Documentação de Estudos em Lingüística Teórica e Aplicada* 13: 159–194.

Dirven, René and Vilém Fried. (1987). 'By way of introduction'. In René Dirven and Vilém Fried (Eds.), *Functionalism in linguistics* (pp. ix–xvii). Amsterdam/Philadelphia: John Benjamins.

Emeneau, Murray B. (1988). 'Bloomfield and Pāṇini'. *Language* 64(4): 755–760.

Foolen, Ad. (2002). [Review of the book *Language form and language function*]. *Functions of Language* 9(1): 87–103.

Francis, Elaine J. (2002). [Review of the book *Language form and language function*]. *Language Sciences* 24: 29–56.

Givón, Talmy. (1995). *Functionalism and grammar*. Amsterdam/Philadelphia: John Benjamins.

Givón, Talmy. (2002). *Biolinguistics: The Santa Barbara lectures.* Amsterdam/ Philadelphia: John Benjamins.

Givón, Talmy. (2013). 'On the intellectual roots of functionalism in linguistics'. In Shannon T. Bischoff and Carmen Jany (Eds.), *Functional approaches to language* (pp. 9–29). Berlin: Walter de Gruyter.

Gleason, Henry Allan. (1961). *An introduction to descriptive linguistics* (Rev. ed.). New York: Holt, Rinehart and Winston.

Graffi, Giorgio. (2001). *200 Years of syntax: A critical survey.* Amsterdam/Philadelphia: John Benjamins.

Halliday, Michael A. K. (1999). 'The notion of "context" in language education'. In Mohsen Ghadessy (Ed.), *Text and context in functional linguistics* (pp. 1–24). Amsterdam/Philadelphia: John Benjamins.

Haspelmath, Martin. (2000). 'Why can't we talk to each other?' [Review of the book *Language form and language function*]. *Lingua* 110: 235–255.

Hockett, Charles F. (1954). 'Two models of grammatical description'. *Word* 10(2–3): 210–234.

Hockett, Charles F. (1958). *A course in modern linguistics.* New York: Macmillan.

Hymes, Dell and John Fought. (1981). *American structuralism.* The Hague: Mouton.

Jakobson, Roman. (1965). 'Quest for the essence of language'. *Diogenes* 13(51): 21–37.

Joseph, John E. (2000). *Limiting the arbitrary: Linguistic naturalism and its opposites in Plato's Cratylus and modern theories of language.* Amsterdam/Philadelphia: John Benjamins.

Joseph, John E. (2002). 'Bloomfield's and Chomsky's readings of the *Cours de linguistique générale*'. In John E. Joseph (Ed.), *From Whitney to Chomsky: Essays in the history of American linguistics* (pp. 133–155). Amsterdam/Philadelphia: John Benjamins.

Katre, Sumitra Mangesh. (1987). Aṣṭādhyāyī *of Pāṇini.* Austin, TX: University of Texas.

Martinet, André. (1962). *A functional view of language.* Oxford: Clarendon Press.

Morpurgo Davies, Anna. (1998). *History of linguistics, volume IV: Nineteenth-century linguistics.* New York: Addison Wesley Longman.

Morvacsik, Edith. (2000). [Review of the book *Language form and language function*]. *Language* 76: 168–170.

Newmeyer, Frederick J. (1998). *Language form and language function.* Cambridge, MA: MIT Press.

Newmeyer, Frederick J. (2001). 'The Prague school and North American functionalist approaches to syntax'. *Journal of Linguistics* 37(1): 101–126.

Pike, Kenneth L. (1954–1960). *Language in relation to a unified theory of the structure of human behavior.* Glendale, CA: Summer Institute of Linguistics. 2nd rev. ed., 1967. The Hague: Mouton.

Sapir, Edward. (1949). 'Language'. In David G. Mandelbaum (Ed.), *Selected writings of Edward Sapir* (pp. 7–32). (Original text published 1933 in *Encyclopedia of the Social Sciences.* Vol. 9, pp. 155–169. New York: Macmillan)

Saussure, Ferdinand de. (1983). *Course in general linguistics* (Charles Bally and Albert Sechehaye, Eds.; Roy Harris, Trans.). London: Duckworth. (Original text published 1916)

Staal, J. F. (Ed.). (1972). *Reader on the Sanskrit grammarians*. Cambridge, MA: MIT Press.

Tallerman, Maggie. (2000). [Review of the book *Language form and language function*]. *Studies in Language* 24: 423–439.

Thomas, Margaret. (2009). [Review of the book *Cartesian Linguistics* (3rd ed.)]. *Language and History* 52: 201–204.

Toman, Jindřich. (1995). *The magic of a common language: Jakobson, Mathesius, Trubetzkoy, and the Prague Linguistic Circle*. Cambridge, MA: MIT Press.

Vachek, Josef. (1967). *A Prague School reader in linguistics*. Bloomington, IN: Indiana University Press.

Van Valin, Robert D., Jr. (2007). 'Some thoughts on the reasons for the lesser status of typology in the USA as opposed to Europe'. *Linguistic Typology* 11: 253–257.

3 Contemporary Formalist Linguistics

3.1 The Internal Structure of Modern Formalism

Contemporary formalist and functionalist linguistics are both animated and contentious intellectual communities, but their internal organization differs starkly. Formalist linguistics from the 1960s to the present day is unusual in that it centers on the output of a single scholar, Noam Chomsky. Chomskyan generative theory is controversial—even among formalists—but its influence is pervasive, especially in the United States, in the sense that even those who oppose Chomsky tend to define their own work relative to his. Chomsky's is the first name, and frequently the only name, that American non-linguists identify with the discipline. His stature is more fraught in Europe, but since the 1970s there have been proponents of Chomskyan formalism at major centers for the study of linguistics, even where they do not form a majority (Haider, Prinzhorn, & van Riemsdijk 1987). The professional organization Generative Linguists of the Old World ('GLOW') specifically fosters research in the generative tradition among European linguists. Founded in Amsterdam, GLOW has sponsored a newsletter and a lively annual conference continuously since 1978. Moreover, generative theory has a strong independent presence in Korea and in Japan (Fukui & Saito 1994).

Granted the centripetal structure of modern formalist linguistics, it makes sense to start Chapter 3 at that center. Section 3.2 sketches out 60 years of Chomskyan formalist linguistics. Section 3.3 expands the tableau by examining modern formalist linguistic theories which depart from generativism while still remaining recognizably formalist.

3.2 What Makes Modern Formalism Formalist?

Chomsky has been an industrious, creative, and fully engaged scholar for more than 60 years. The convention is to divide his output into stages, which are roughly internally coherent, but which have to be studied with the understanding that incremental shifts took place in his thinking at many points, so that ideas from one stage have bled into adjacent stages. We will ground discussion of what is formalist in Chomskyan formal linguistics in a conventional three-stage chronology anchored by some of his major publications: in subsection 3.2.1, early transformational grammar (Chomsky 1957, 1965); in 3.2.2, principles and parameters (Chomsky 1984, 1986); and in 3.2.3, the Minimalist Program (Chomsky 1995, 2000).

My goal is not to give a full explication of Chomsky's linguistics, since many such expositions already exist, at various levels of detail—and readers of this text may be familiar with at least some version of generative theory. Rather, my goal in section 3.2 is to narrate the development of generative theory from 1957 to the early twenty-first century with reference to how its specifically formalist character has evolved over the years.

3.2.1 Early Transformational Grammar

Chomsky studied as an undergraduate at the University of Pennsylvania under American structuralist Zellig Harris (1909–1992), absorbing from him many of the traits of the linguistics of the day: conceptualization of the discipline as a science; the assumption that a grammar is a concise specification of the structure of a language; concern for methodology. According to Derwing (1980), Chomsky adopted from Bloomfield (likely via Harris) the core formalist notion that language can be analyzed an autonomous system of formal rules—autonomous from the context of its use by speakers and hearers, and autonomous from related disciplines. On the other hand, Chomsky strongly rejected Bloomfieldian behaviorism, and asserted that a grammar should be modeled on speakers' intuitions about acceptable versus unacceptable utterances, rather than on a corpus of attested utterances. Insiders to generative grammar consider this to constitute a sharp rupture with American structuralism, using the terms 'revolution' or 'paradigm shift' to describe its emergence in a disciplinary context dominated by post-Bloomfieldian linguistics (Joseph 1995). However, Chomskyan generative linguistics has at least its formalist character—present from Chomsky's earliest publications—in common with its direct disciplinary ancestors.

Chomsky compiled *Syntactic Structures* (1957) from his notes for an introductory course in linguistics that he taught to MIT engineers and mathematicians. His goal was to disabuse them of their assumption that a grammar could be conceived of as the output of a finite-state machine. A finite-state machine is a simple computational model, often represented as a flow chart comprising boxes and arrows connected at nodes which stand for decision points. At each decision point, input from the environment selects one of a limited number of options, which leads to a predetermined subsequent state. The machine cannot 'look back' to earlier states or decision points, nor does it anticipate what lies ahead. In place of this limited and mechanical model for the structure of human language, Chomsky introduced the notion of a three-component grammar, consisting of a set of phrase structure rules that generate 'kernel sentences'; freely containing abstract elements like 'PAST' or 'AUX(ILIARY)' as the economy of the analysis demands; transformational rules that operate on the output of phrase structure rules by copying, moving, and deleting elements of the kernel sentences; and morphophonemic rules that derive surface forms from the output of the transformational component, such as replacing '*sing* + PAST' with '*sang*'.

In *Aspects of the Theory of Syntax* (1965) Chomsky developed a wider context for his ideas, discussing competence/performance; linguistic universals (as his use of the expression 'universal grammar' emerged); deep structure/surface structure; acceptability versus grammaticality; description versus explanation; the organization of 'the base' (input to the transformational component) and of the lexicon. Throughout, Chomsky's stance is resolutely formalist. His linguistic theory defines the inner structure of human language, which assumes the autonomy of syntax from semantics and discourse, the autonomy of grammar from general cognitive faculties, and the central importance of studying what people know about language (their competence) as opposed to the degraded expression of that knowledge evident in what people say (their performance). Chomsky proposed that a grammar comprises independent modules that interact with each other, so that although speakers' syntactic knowledge comes to bear on their phonological competence, the two can be studied separately. In *Aspects*, Chomsky identified the primitive units of the syntactic component according to their forms, as 'noun' or 'preposition', rather than relationally as 'subject', 'predicate', or 'object'. His argument against what he called those 'functional notions' was that most of what they contribute to grammatical analysis can be derived directly from formal configurational relationships (1965: 68–74), therefore to admit them into a grammar is redundant. In a footnote, Chomsky further rejected the notions of 'topic' and 'comment'—terms fundamental to many functionalist analyses—on a similar basis: a topic is 'the leftmost NP that is immediately dominated by S in the surface structure and that is, furthermore, a major [syntactic] category' (1965: 221). Moreover, from the beginning of his career Chomsky has employed idealized, decontextualized data, both grammatical and ungrammatical, to illustrate the operation of the system (e.g., *Sincerity frightens the boy; *The boy frightens sincerity*).

It is worthwhile reviewing one of the most memorable, and most glamorous, of Chomsky's early-period proposals, 'Affix-hopping' (Lasnik 2000). All parts of it have been superseded by his subsequent theorizing, but it still stands as a remarkable museum piece of late 1950s formalist style. Affix-hopping—technically, the 'Auxiliary Transformation' (1957: 113)—names a transformation in English grammar that governs the distribution of auxiliaries and the heterogeneous forms of the verb *write* in sentences like those in (1a—f).

(1) a. Camila writes for the *Globe*
    b. Camila is writing for the *Globe*
    c. Camila wrote for the *Globe*
    d. Camila has written for the *Globe*
    e. Camila has been writing for the *Globe*
    f. Camila could have been writing for the *Globe*

Chomsky generalized pre-verbal markers for tense and aspect into a single category 'Af[fix]', and identified auxiliary *have, be, do*, modals, and lexical verbs as members of a category he called 'v'. The operation of Affix-hopping attaches any member of 'Af' onto the end of the next adjacent 'v', iteratively, from left to right. That is to say, (1d) derives from the deep structure represented in (2a), which contains two affixes: an abstract tense marker PRES[ent], and *en*, which is part of the abstract perfect aspect marker *have + en*. The transformation Affix-hopping applies to (2a), yielding (2b). The relevant morphophonemic rules then apply to (2b) to produce the pronounceable forms (*Camila*) *has written* (*for the Globe*).

(2) a. Camila PRES have en write for the *Globe*
    b. Camila have.PRES write.en for the *Globe*

Affix-hopping interacts with a '*Do* Transformation', which inserts expletive *do* in contexts where no 'v' appears to the left of an affix. In the derivation of the negative sentence *Camila did not write for the* Globe, (3a) shows that the affix PAST cannot 'hop' to the right, because the next adjacent word, *not*, is not a member of the class of 'v'. In (3b) the *Do* Transformation inserts *do* to rescue the stranded affix. After the relevant morphophonemic rules apply, the outcome is (*Camila*) *did not write* (*for the* Globe), with the past tense marker realized on *do* rather than on *write*.

(3) a. Camila PAST not write for the *Globe*
    b. Camila do.PAST not write for the *Globe*

Virtually none of the particulars in these early drafts of Chomsky's ideas has survived into subsequent versions of generative grammar. However, their bold formalism is consistent with later developments: grammar is a set of precise operations, sometimes involving abstract forms that are remote from what we perceive in normal speech, which can be studied independent of how speakers use language (i.e., how speakers build their identities, express perceptions, exchange messages). Needless to say, a functionalist's point of view on the phenomenon of Affix-Hopping would bring very different issues to light: the salience of the employment of *do* in the context of negation; the communicative significance of the fact that negation adds rather than takes material away. A functionalist point of view might also take on other challenges, such as accounting for the role of language processing granted that English tense markers precede aspect markers, while verbs follow auxiliary elements. Goldberg and Del Giudice (2005), for example, present functional motivations for the related construction of subject-auxiliary inversion (e.g., *Does Camila write for the* Globe?).

3.2.2　Principles and Parameters

A second stage in the development of generative grammar significantly increased its scope and sophistication, and the ambition of the theory to account for what makes human languages both resemble and differ from each other. By 1980, Chomsky had survived major challenges to his work, and had attracted a cohort of colleagues and students who were assiduously extending generative concepts and tools to new languages and to new niches of familiar languages. Writing from within this dynamic, internally contentious research program, Chomsky (1984, 1986) proposed that a grammar can be construed as a set of universal principles intrinsic to a human language faculty, which include specific points of parametric variation. Learners select from limited parametric options embedded in those principles, on the evidence of their observations of the surrounding language; those options govern the differences between, say, Italian and Spanish or Italian and Cherokee. The goal was to account for ways that human grammars vary structurally, by conceiving of them as consequences of a limited inventory of parameter settings.

A generative grammar capable of meeting these goals required building up an extensive theoretical apparatus fine-tuned to accommodate cross-linguistic differences. Among proposals developed in this interval were constraints on syntactic movement, including Subjacency; locality conditions; syntactic chains; binding theory; the inventory of empty categories and their properties; overt and covert case-marking; c-command and government; theta-marking; the Projection Principle; traces; X-bar theory; and the distinction between I(nternal)-language versus E(xternal)-language. (An alternative label for this stage of Chomsky's theorizing, 'government and binding', refers to two key proposals.) For our purposes what is more important than either the content of these notions, or their longevity versus ephemerality, is the fact of their consistently formalist architecture. The apparatus of principles and parameters maintained its focus on the form of language, not discourse, not a speaker's expressive choices, and not semantics that went beyond judgments of, say, the scope of negation in two utterances or whether two sentences are synonymous.

variationist sociophonetician' (p. 373). Although the main business of the text is to assess the books under review while giving voice to both formalist and functionalist readings of them, there is an arc to the conversation. It begins with playful name-calling, in which Carnie labels Mendoza-Denton with the same epithet that Newmeyer's Forman directs at Funk—'fuzzy'—while Mendoza-Denton echoes Funk's term for Forman ('symbol pusher') in a swipe at Carnie's devotion to 'contentless formalisms'. But the two parties move on to discover some signs of compatibility, on the evidence from the conference papers that in phonology, at least, both formalist and functionalist evidence is salient. From there, Carnie and Mendoza-Denton proceed, circuitously, to grudging acceptance of shared assessments of some of the papers and of shared stances (that syntax can be said to, at least, interact with discourse; that synchronic variation may initiate diachronic change; that both functional pressures and formal structural properties have implications for typology). In the end they resolve that, after all, formalists and functionalists may not be so far apart: 'it seems like a lot of the "debate" about formalism and functionalism revolves around people characterizing each other's positions in extreme terms, setting up unrealistic expectations' (p. 387).

Carnie and Mendoza-Denton's review makes a tidy narrative—a conversion story of sorts—that locates formalists versus functionalists differently relative to each other, compared to the stalemate in which Newmeyer's Forman and Funk are locked. Neither tableau seems unrealistic. There likely have been actual conversations between differently oriented linguists who, if they have the patience to walk through evidence bearing on formalism versus functionalism together, converge in their views more than they had anticipated without abandoning the perspectives they started from. Carnie and Mendoza-Denton's sketch models this benign outcome. There are, however, other imaginable positions that formalists and functionalists could take relative to each other: positions from which—in the popular folkloristic terms—'symbol pushers' unilaterally criticize 'fuzzies' or vice versa; from which one side asserts ownership of the other's achievements; or from which the two come to view their goals as incompatible and their differences too extensive to be reconciled.

6.2.2 How Formal Is Functionalism?

Continuing with our agenda to eavesdrop on exchanges between the two parties (but shifting from imaginary conversations to published literature), in this subsection we listen to how formalists have talked back to functionalists. A matter of particular interest is formalists' claims that functionalists have converged toward formalism or appropriated quasi-formalist claims and assumptions.

We know that formalism and functionalism differ in many ways: in their conception of the fundamental nature of language with respect to communication and cognition; in their essential theoretical constructs; in their methodological practices and treatment of data; in how they organize a grammar; in their relationships with other disciplines; in their typical working habits. With these dimensions of difference in mind, and moreover recalling the heterogeneity of modern functionalism, one might expect formalist critiques of functionalism to be both many and diverse. In fact, formalists engage in less analysis of the faults of functionalism than one might expect, and what critique they do offer is surprisingly convergent.

An exception to this generalization is Frederick Newmeyer, a scholar who has written extensively about formalism and functionalism (1991, 1992, 1998, 1999, 2003, 2005a, 2005c). Although Newmeyer is a formalist by training and commitment, he happily adopts the characterization 'functionalist Chomskyan' (2005a: 232). He has looked critically and in depth into the conceptual basis and empirical research on both sides. His conclusion is that there is little principled incompatibility between them. On the way to that conclusion, a theme in his writing is that functionalism is more consistent with formalism than it may appear to be. That is to say, Newmeyer is quick to identify formalist-like traits within functionalism, or at least traits not threatening to formalism, and quick to undercut facets of functionalism that challenge formalism.

An example of this comes to light in his treatment of a core principle of formalism, autonomy. Newmeyer (1998: 23–94) places autonomy at the center of his formalist's-eye-view of the debate. He begins his exposition by defining three partially independent hypotheses about autonomy to which many formalists adhere: (1) that syntax is autonomous from semantics and discourse; (2) that competence is autonomous from performance, and from 'the social, cognitive, and communicative factors contributing to use [of competence]' (p. 24); and (3) that grammar is autonomous from general cognition.

Functionalists do not necessarily accept any of these notions of autonomy. But from Newmeyer's point of view, functionalist research that questions (1) through (3), ultimately fails to debunk the autonomy hypotheses. For example, with respect to (1), Goldberg's Cognitive Construction Grammar identifies the central use of the English ditransitive construction 'V NP NP' (*Sally baked her sister a cake*; Goldberg 1995: 141–151) as involving transfer of an object by a volitional agent to a willing recipient; speakers then extend the construction to sanction its metaphorical use, as in *The music lent the party a festive air*. Newmeyer, however, denies that the association which Goldberg asserts between syntax and meaning threatens the autonomy of syntax: 'simply showing that there is an intimate relationship between form and meaning or even that metaphors have grammatical consequences is not sufficient to defeat [(1)]' (1998: 45).

Likewise, Newmeyer denies that Hopper's notion of emergent grammar undermines (2), the autonomy of competence and performance. Emergent grammar claims that there is no 'competence' in the sense that language has no independent existence outside of specific discourse acts. Instead, it is made of prefabricated parts which speakers put together improvisationally. Newmeyer (pp. 59–64) objects that it is unclear how children could learn a language comprised of bits and pieces encountered incidentally—or how to account for uniformity in the course of child language acquisition. With respect to (3), Newmeyer turns up functionalists who, on his reading, either support the autonomy of grammar from general cognition (Givón); are agnostic (Langacker); or reject it while asserting what amounts only to an apparent counter-position, that study of language should be informed by cognitive psychology and neuroscience (Lakoff).

Therefore, according to Newmeyer, functionalists either do not succeed in repudiating the bedrock formalist assumptions (1) through (3), or do not try to repudiate them. In a 1992 article, he took a similar approach on the topic of iconicity, with which many functionalists oppose formalist assumptions about arbitrariness. Newmeyer makes three arguments: that iconicity is irrelevant to generative grammar; that (in any case) iconicity poses no challenge to generative grammar; and that iconicity is already presupposed in some versions of generative grammar (1992: 756). He examines data and arguments put forth by most of the functionalist pantheon mentioned in Chapter 4, but reaches a conclusion about iconicity that parallels his conclusion about autonomy, namely, that functionalists fall not all that far from formalists.

Not all readers agree, however. In commentary on Newmeyer, Hopper objected to what he sees as Newmeyer's assimilation of functionalism into formalism: he characterized Newmeyer as 'tr[ying] to interpret "functionalism" in terms of the formalist paradigm' (1991: 46). Hopper might have the same reaction to an essay by Anderson in the proceedings of the University of Wisconsin–Milwaukee conference. Anderson's assignment was to comment on 'what formalists can learn from functionalists in syntax' (1999: 112). His answer is, essentially, 'not much', since he finds little in functionalism that disrupts his formalist outlook. Most tellingly, what exceptions Anderson admits are instances where functionalism conforms to formalism: 'some functionalist work is in fact close enough to that of your canonical formalist to make dialogue and reciprocal interaction fairly straightforward' (p. 118). Note that Anderson's syntax specifies that it is the approach of functionalism to formalism that facilitates dialogue—not mutual rapprochement, and not a movement of formalism in the direction of functionalism. Anderson cites as an example Kuno's research on empathy, research which (as we saw in Chapter 4) is usually classified on the far edge of functionalism abutting formalism. That is, Anderson comes closest to investing value in functionalism when it speaks to him in formalist terms. In assessing functionalism, the question he asks is: 'How *formalist* is functionalism?'

At the risk of overstating the point, one might notice that there are other options. Croft (1995), like Newmeyer, discusses the issue of autonomy. He defines a number of positions linguists have taken with respect to the autonomy of syntax, of grammar, and of language, noting that some seem to mix formalist and functionalist stances. He cites an analysis of Babungo, spoken in Cameroon, where noun class agreement phenomena are partially syntactic, and (in an apparent challenge to the autonomy of syntax) partially assigned by semantic or discourse factors. Croft asserts that it is possible to 'smuggle' semantics into syntax by replicating the relevant semantic features in the syntactic component (pp. 501–503). What is salient in Croft's presentation of this problem, and its proposed solution, is that he conceives of it as part of a 'near-continuum of [formalist] and functionalist theories' (p. 526) rather than as an assimilation of one to the other, or an attempt to interpret one in the terms of the other.

It remains to be determined what kind of account provides more insight into the nature of language: a mixed account that admits 'smuggling' across the border between syntax and semantics; a formalist one that prohibits 'smuggling' on principle; or a functionalist one that denies that there is such a border. Anderson (1999: 127–129) comments on Croft's Babungo data, remarking that he finds in it no challenge to a strictly formalist account. In his analysis, 'smuggling' need not take place: general principles of agreement which also operate between modifiers and heads, or between verbs and their arguments, govern the syntactic components of Babungo agreement. Whatever residue of agreement is controlled by semantics and discourse is 'not at all a matter of sentence syntax' (p. 128) and would be accounted for elsewhere in the grammar. With that, Anderson implicitly rejects Croft's notion of a continuum between formalism and functionalism. By extracting for separate treatment just those facets of the Babungo data that are amenable to formal analysis while setting aside facets that depend on semantics or discourse, he supplants Croft's 'mixed' functional proposal with a purely formalist analysis.

Another criticism that has been directed at functionalists has a different status. Many, including Anderson, have complained that functionalist texts are marred by inexplicit, vague, intuitive, or obscure language in the place of formalized terms and concepts (Labov 1987: 313;

Anderson 1999: 11, 115, 120; Newmeyer 2001: 114–116)—leading, fairly or not, to the epithet 'fuzzy'. Anderson does not consider inadequate formalization intrinsic to functionalism, but simply a too-common practice among those who take that approach. Formalists, of course, value their trademark style of explicit definitions and axioms, which, in their eyes, renders their ideas clear and unambiguous. Insofar as adequately formalizing a claim means simply expressing it with clarity and precision, that ideal should transcend differences between the two approaches. The tricky part lies in adjudicating what counts as adequately precise language. As Hengeveld (1999) points out, some varieties of functionalism, such as Foley and Van Valin's Role and Reference Grammar (1984) and Dik's functional grammar (1978, 1989), formalize their proposals in their own idiosyncratic, intrinsically functionalist, idioms which still aspire to the kind of explicitness that formalists value. For other functionalists (Halliday, Givón) formalization is not a priority: for them, clarity and precision are achieved by other means. For still other functionalists, the critique misfires: 'functional research has been severely held back by inappropriate or premature demands for rigor, abstractness, generality, and so on, stated as absolute, a priori criteria of science' (Beaugrade 1994: 176).

6.2.3 How Functionalist Is Formalism?

In short, much of formalist critique seeks to reconcile functionalism in the direction of formalism. Now we hand the microphone over to functionalists: how have they talked back to formalists?

The overall tenor of functionalist critique of formalism is, unsurprisingly, more heterogeneous than the converse body of critique. It is also more profuse. In general, functionalists seem more self-conscious about tension between their ideas and those of formalists than vice versa (a point to which we return in section 6.4).

Some functionalists comment in depth on formalism and on the gap between it and their own work. Other functionalists are more restrained in their objections to formalist policies and practices. Halliday belongs to this second group: he tended to put forth his own ideas rather than argue against views he rejected. But a critique is present nonetheless. For example, in discussing the labeling of grammatical categories, Halliday emphasized in the following passage that systemic functional linguistics does not start with an inventory of ready-made labels or concepts (like 'theme' or 'NP').

> . . . we do not use the name to impose artificial rigour on a language. Linguistic phenomena tend to be indeterminate, with lots of ambiguities, blends and 'borderline cases'. The categories of analysis take this

into account, allowing us to treat it not as something exceptional or dys-
functional, but as a natural and positive feature of an evolving system.

(Halliday 1992 / 2003: 201)

Halliday tacitly characterized formalist labels as 'impos[ing] artificial
rigour', in opposition to the 'natural and positive' practices of systemic
functional linguistics, which are emergent, flexible, and prototype-centered.
In the same text and through similar rhetorical moves, Halliday dismissed
formalist pursuit of a discipline based on the natural sciences; the sources
and treatment of data typical of formalism; formalist notions of 'explanation'; formalist reification of 'structure' over 'system' (pp. 200–212).

Langacker, on the other hand, tends to be more straightforward in his criticism of formal grammar. About his own cognitive grammar, he wrote that
'Some linguists view it with disdain, as it challenges fundamental dogmas
and requires alternative modes of thought and analysis' (2008: 5). On Halliday's topic of the labeling of grammatical units, he continues, 'Received
wisdom—repeated in every linguistic textbook—holds that notions like
noun and subject are purely grammatical categories not susceptible to any
general semantic characterization', whereas cognitive grammar 'denies this
by claiming that all valid grammatical constructs are symbolic, hence reduc-
ible to form-meaning pairings' (pp. 5–7). In the same passage, Langacker
links the matter to the formalist conception of the autonomy of syntax, to
which he confronts cognitive grammar's conception of 'a gradation consisting solely in assemblies of symbolic structures'. He goes on to counter
'the distorting lens of contemporary linguistic theory'; to mention what he
perceives as a fallacy leading some formalists to exaggerate the scope of
functionalists' claims; and correct the confused understanding that positing
overlap across the lexicon, syntax, and morphology necessarily means that
cognitive grammarians do not distinguish among them. In these ways, Langacker directly engages with formalism, laying explicit boundaries down
between cognitive grammar and opposing approaches.

Givón sometimes takes a more combative tone in his critique of formalism, for example, in his 1979 analysis of 'the threefold methodological delusion' of generative grammar (p. 8); 'the gutting of the database' by
which formalists impoverish linguistics (p. 22); and the 'unprecedented'
synthesis of 'theoretical vacuity' and 'empirical irresponsibility' that comprises Chomsky's proposals (p. 44). However, in other writings—without
retreating from his repudiation of formalism—Givón (1995) argues that
both functionalists and formalists fall into black-and-white thinking that
warrants correction. He details the sources and consequences of numer-
ous extreme positions on both sides, such as the 'naïve functionalism' of
'[b]ecause structure is not 100% arbitrary, it must be 100% iconic'

juxtaposed against equally pernicious 'naïve Platonic reductionism' of '[e]ither all form-function pairings are non-arbitrary, or else functionalism is empirically vacuous' (pp. 10–11).

Against this kaleidoscopic corpus of criticism of the many, by the many, from many directions, it is reasonable to ask whether functionalists, like formalists, see the other party as approaching (or encroaching) on their own positions. The assimilatory stance which formalists sometimes adopt (discussed in subsection 6.2.2) also shows up in functionalist critiques of formalism. An example is Bates and MacWhinney's (1990) response to Pinker and Bloom's (1990) article questioning Chomsky's views on the origin of language. Bates and MacWhinney advert to their idea that there are four levels of increasingly deeper commitment to the ideals of functionalism, starting with a Level 1 which (merely) accepts that communication plays a role in shaping language form at some stage of its historical development. They attribute Level 1 functionalism to Pinker and Bloom on the evidence that, contra Chomsky, Pinker and Bloom argue that natural selection found something to favor in the early emergence of human language, then capitalized on it. Bates and MacWhinney also find evidence elsewhere in Pinker's and Bloom's work of covert Level 3 functionalism, which asserts that children exploit form/function links in acquisition. Their evidence resides in Pinker's (1984) and Bloom's (1990) research showing that children deduce the syntactic properties of words from their meanings via what Pinker called 'semantic bootstrapping'. On this basis, Bates and MacWhinney perceive that Pinker and Bloom are moving away from doctrinaire formalism. On a triumphant note, they title their commentary 'Welcome to Functionalism'.

In their response, Pinker and Bloom deflect the assimilatory welcome, edging away from Bates and MacWhinney. They dryly acknowledge that they do believe that semantics exists and that children make use of semantics in acquiring syntax, but protest that 'it's not clear who isn't a functionalist in this sense' (1990: 740)—including Chomsky. At issue in this exchange seems to be the foundational, unsettled matter of what the autonomy of syntax from semantics means to formalists, to functionalists, and within each side's understanding of the other side's position.

There is also a stream of literature in which functionalists take assimilation to the maximum, to declare victory over formalists. Beaugrade (1994) confidently announces that 'the tide is turning' toward functionalism and that 'I see no way the shift can be postponed if the science of language is to regain some solid footing' (p. 1950). He asserts that 'pure formalism runs aground on its own austere principles and is trapped in irresolvable dilemmas' (p. 177), clearing the way for a full-voiced functionalism that replaces, instead of merely augments, formalism. Geeraerts (2010) announces that cognitive grammar has passed through pioneering and building phases into a stage of consolidation. He provides bibliographical data over a 20-year interval showing an abrupt increase in references to 'cognitive grammar / linguistics', with a correlative decline in references to 'generative grammar / linguistics'. Enfield (2013) asserts that '[u]niversalist, rationalist approaches have recently gone from dominant to outdated', marking the abandonment of 'desiccated and socioculturally impoverished versions of linguistics' (pp. 155). Enfield cites a host of publications as witness.

A less sweeping, but provocative assimilatory claim argues that Chomsky himself has adopted functionalist ideas. Golumbia picks up on traits of the Minimalist Program, which in his eyes mark it as 'hard to distinguish from functionalist theories' (p. 40). As mentioned in Chapter 5, the Minimalist Program raises the profile of the two external interfaces that interact with the formal computational mechanisms of the language faculty 'in the narrow sense': the conceptual-intentional system and the sensory-motor system. Golumbia emphasizes that Chomsky's renewed attention to the coordination of meaning with sound and his radical hollowing out of universal grammar—formerly, the hallmark of generative theory, and a focus for conflict between formalists and functionalists—brings minimalism closer to functionalism.

6.3 Side by Side

A next step is to juxtapose formalism and functionalism laterally, in the sense of examining issues that bear equally on both approaches, and that may help us see where each stands relative to the other. Among issues that could be explored fruitfully in this way, two are conspicuous. The first is the fraught matter of explanation: how do formalists versus functionalists explain why the facts of language are what they are? What counts as an 'explanation' under each of these two approaches? The second issue is the question of complementarity: can formalism and functionalism be brought together in some way, so that each complements the other to provide a fuller account of the nature of language? Or do they compete for a unique role within a limited conceptual space?

6.3.1 Explanation

The capacity to explain why the shape of language is what it is, is crucial to both formalists and functionalists. The two approaches rival each other, side by side, in laying claim to the prestige of being able to explain language facts. They also stand side by side in viewing their counterparts' explanations skeptically. The issue is sufficiently developed that a matched pair of terms have emerged: formalists pursue 'internal' explanations, and functionalists 'external' explanations.

Generativists hold a proprietary relationship with the notion of explanation going back to Chomsky (1965: 30–37). In distancing himself from his formalist predecessors, Chomsky articulated three ascending levels of adequacy that a grammar must achieve. A grammar that meets the criterion of 'observational adequacy', accurately labels language data; 'descriptive adequacy', specifies the rules that generate those data; and 'explanatory adequacy', gives principled reasons for valuing one possible grammar over another, and makes predictions that go beyond the observed data. In pursuing the ideal of explanatory adequacy, Chomsky reacted against an austere streak in post-Bloomfieldian linguistics which abjured any departure from description to try to explain language facts: the post-Bloomfieldian Martin Joos (1907–1978) famously remarked that 'Children want explanations, and there is a child in each of us; descriptivism makes a virtue of not pampering that child' (1958: 96). Generativists explicitly reject that posture by aiming to explain the facts of language within terms of their own theory. In fact, prioritizing explanation over description is often identified as a distinguishing feature of generative theory.

As an example of what it means to explain language facts from a formalist perspective within the terms of generative theory, recall Hyams's (1999) account of children's telegraphic speech. Her data showed that 83% of verbs that child learners left unmarked for finiteness appeared with null subjects, compared to 23% of verbs with finite inflections. Moving from observation to description, Hyams generalized the notion of (non-)finiteness from verbs to nouns, drawing on generative theory's disposition to discover symmetry across syntactic classes. She proposed that young children generate non-finite verbs (verbs lacking inflectional features) in the context of non-finite nouns (which include null subjects, and nouns lacking determiners or plural markers). From here Hyams went on to seek an explanation for why finiteness correlates across verbal and nominal domains in child language, granted that this is not a property of the adult grammar. She recruited a proposal from then-current generative grammar that identified the heads of functional categories as pronominal in nature and therefore underspecified. She invoked a principle that blocks the construal of pronominals pragmatically when an anaphoric option is available. Adults acquire this principle as they gain expertise in language use, as it is not part of universal grammar. Until children acquire it, they allow pragmatic construal of pronominals in telegraphic speech.

It is worthwhile reflecting on the structure of Hyams's argument as an example of what it means to explain an observation about child language within generative theory. Notice that her explanation is built within a dense network of theory-internal proposals: about cross-categorical symmetry; about the pronominal character of the heads of functional categories; about the interaction of grammatical and pragmatic principles, with the latter driven by environmental learning and the former by universal grammar. One might add that Hyams's starting point is also part of the explanation, in that *ab initio* she is disposed to expect children's performance with functional categories to under-represent their actual competence. Hyams's explanation for telegraphic speech is internal in the sense that it rests on an elaborate tissue of interlocking theory-internal proposals. Insofar as these proposals successfully hang together in the explanation of multiple linguistic facts, so far the whole apparatus of generative theory is strengthened.

It should also be noted that internal explanation in generative theory often invokes the innateness of universal grammar (Hoekstra & Kooji 1988). In the case at hand, Hyams assumes that child learners bring intact to the context of learning elaborate, abstract knowledge about functional categories and their properties, knowledge that cannot be attributed to general cognitive skills. All that they need to learn from environmental input is the pragmatic principle that anaphoric identification of a pronominal preempts its identification through discourse. The readiness of formalists to locate elaborate, abstract knowledge of language in an innate language faculty is, of course, a point of maximum contention with functionalists. For many functionalists, to say that 'XYZ is innate' does not and cannot serve as an explanation for the existence of XYZ; it merely articulates an unsupported claim. In the words of Givón, 'without reference to *function* and *evolution* no explanation of the structural properties of an organism is possible' (1979: 22; emphasis in the original).

Givón's objection to the role that generativists assign to innateness (which many have developed: Derwing 1973: 63–77; Sampson 2005; Fischer 2007: 71–74) appears in an extended rebuke of their conception of what counts as an explanation for linguistic facts (1979: 3–22). The gist of Givón's complaint is that formalism rules out *a priori* what seem to him to be the obvious, compelling sources of explanation: meaning, discourse pragmatics, processing constraints, human cognitive structure, diachronic change, and so forth. All of these are touchstones of functionalism's conception of how to explain language. In their place, according to Givón, formalists create an artificial model of language, dub it a 'theory', and then invest that theory with explanatory power.

Pivoting now to focus on functionalist conceptions of explanation, functionalists—like their formalist counterparts—also claim special insight into explanation. But the grounds on which they do so differ. Insofar as functionalists interpret the motto 'form follows function' to mean that function imposes a shape on language forms, then the relevance of exactly those forces that formalists reject come into play: meaning, discourse pragmatics, processing constraints, human cognitive structure, diachronic change, etc. (Notice that the conventional characterization of these forces as 'external', privileges a formalist view of them, in the sense that they are external to the core language faculty. From a functionalist point of view, meaning, discourse, processing, etc., are 'internal', not 'external', factors.) Speaking for functionalism, Payne (1999: 142–143) provides a memorable analogy. Holding up a (randomly chosen, unremarkable) leaf she asks, '*Why* is this leaf flat?' A formalist might respond that the leaf is flat because more of its cells are arranged in one dimension than in the other. According to Payne, this 'explanation' misfires because it merely re-describes what it means to be 'flat'. Another formalist may respond that the leaf is flat because of its genes; this corresponds to the invocation of innateness. A functionalist, on the other hand, might respond that the leaf is flat because flatness is functional: flatness enhances the leaf's exposure to sunlight, which therefore increases photosynthesis. To Payne, only this third response is truly explanatory: leaves are flat because their form follows their function of converting light into chemical energy.

Newmeyer (2005c: 174–175) digs deeper into form and function in distinguishing two views of their relationship in the context of explanation. Some functionalists seek evidence directly connecting specific functions to specific forms; others connect functions indirectly to forms through constraints on acquisition and language change. The first option Newmeyer calls 'atomistic functionalism', the second 'holistic functionalism'. Although Newmeyer concedes a place for 'holistic functionalism' in which functional pressures act indirectly on form, he rejects atomistic functionalism, which is prevalent in functionalist literature. He gives as an example Dik's (1989: 215) analysis of English ditransitive sentences, which asserts that form connects directly to function in ditransitive structures. In *The man gave the book to the boy*, form reflects the functional principle of iconicity, since the order of major elements in the sentence represents the actual transaction originating in the agent (*man*), who transmits the object (*book*) into the possession of the recipient (*boy*). Moreover, according to Dik, form also reflects function in the alternative sentence, *The man gave the boy the book*, in the guise of a principle that prioritizes the animate, human noun *boy* over an inanimate *book*.

In this way, atomistic functionalism purports to link every element in grammar point-by-point to a functional motivation. Newmeyer objects that in atomistic functionalism the scope of potential motivations is large, and indeterminant: iconicity, prototypicality, markedness, prominence, topic maintenance, focus, economy, parsing ease, memory constraints, and many other factors have been nominated. Functionalists may be at ease with such an open-ended inventory of explanatory instruments. In the language of Payne's metaphor, some leaves are flatter (or larger, differently shaped, differently colored) than others because behind the full scope of forms lies a large inventory of explanatory functions, including maximizing photosynthesis; shade; rainfall; humidity; length of the growing season, etc. For functionalists, this is all grist for the mill. But many formalist critics agree with Lass (1980: 70), who remarked (in a discussion of functional explanation for language change) on the 'virtual invulnerability of functional arguments' in that '[t]he trouble with arguments like this is that you can't lose'.

As a final example of what emerges in comparing formalist and functionalist conceptions of explanation side by side, some functionalists have elaborated on generative grammar's notion of explanatory adequacy. Initiated by Dik (1989), Butler (2003, Part 2: 485–489) exploded Chomsky's idea of three levels of adequacy with the goal of explaining 'why the language we describe is as it is' under a new, expanded, definition of explanatory adequacy. To Butler, a grammar that explains language must meet criteria of discoursal adequacy (taking into account authentic, dynamic data produced by speakers in particular relations to each other); sociocultural adequacy (with reference to the relevant social and cultural environment, and the immediate environment of the preceding discourse); psychological/cognitive adequacy (taking on processing; inferencing; the mental representation of communicative intentions); and acquisitional adequacy (grammars must show how children acquire not only the core grammar and lexicon, but how they arrive at the norms for discourse in the language). With this enlarged list of desiderata, Butler mapped out an ambitious, maximally external, functionalist notion of what counts as an explanation. It contrasts with a formalist notion of explanation such as that assumed by Hyams, which looks inward to assess the theory-internal coherence and consistency of a claim for why language is what it is.

6.3.2 *(Non)complementarity*

Surveying the mutual criticism of formalism and functionalism, and working through their contrasting notions of what counts as an explanation, sharpens our sense of how the two parties differ. In this subsection we continue to juxtapose the two side by side to ask what kinds of relationships might hold between them: if not harmony, at least complementarity—or not. As it turns out, there is no consensus about how to position formalism and functionalism relative to each other. But it is important to understand the range of positions that participants in the debate take.

Among attempts to articulate a complementary relationship between formalism and functionalism, one position acknowledges the different domains of their concerns while incorporating the formalist conception of modularity. This is the stance of 'formal' or 'conservative' functionalists, who assign functional factors to a separate component of the grammar. Kuno makes the point clear:

> given a linguistic process that is governed by both syntactic and, say, discourse factors, the syntactic aspect will be formulated in the syntactic component, while discourse factors will be described in the discourse component of the grammar. . . . There need not be any disagreement between the two.
>
> (Kuno 1987: 1)

In fact, this position seems to be tacitly assumed by some formalists *tout court*. Recall that Hyams (1999) invokes a pragmatic principle which interacts with children's grammatical competence to account for telegraphic speech. Hyams's concern is with grammatical competence, and she presupposes the autonomy of syntax from pragmatics. Therefore she can incorporate that pragmatic principle into her argument, adopting Kuno's no-disagreement stance.

Kuno and Takami (1993: 165) urge linguists to be on the lookout for points like this where syntactic factors interact with discourse or pragmatics. They criticize generativists for proposing purely formal accounts of phenomena that they feel can be better accounted for by the interaction of syntactic and functional constraints. Among those phenomena, Kuno and Takami include Heavy NP Shift, reflexives in picture nouns, and sentences with multiple WH words. Formal functionalists extend formalist methodology and practices to data analysis: they assume the sentence is the basic unit of analysis; freely idealize language data; rely on native speaker intuitions; downplay inter-speaker variation. They are undisturbed by the epistemological gaps between formalism and functionalism, and remain serenely confident that the two approaches, though distinct, can work together to make the best account of linguistic patterns.

A different stance on the complementarity of formalism and functionalism appears in the work of Newmeyer. He staunchly defends the compatibility of the two on the grounds that grammar can be both autonomous and externally motivated (1998: 365–369, 1999: 469, 2005b: 277–278). Earlier in this chapter, we reviewed his claims that functionalism is more consistent with formalism than it may at first appear. In addition to this perception, Newmeyer sees the same developments in the Minimalist Program and biolinguistics that Golumbia (2008) remarked on as evidence of incipient compatibility between formalism and functionalism. Among that evidence, Newmeyer includes erosion of a commitment to the autonomy of syntax—which he laments (2005b:

278–279)—and Chomsky's (2005) recognition of the 'third factor', that is, the importance of principles not specific to language that bear on language design.

It is important to recognize that the purported convergence of recent generative grammar with functionalism does not resemble Kuno's deliberate revision of formalism to accommodate functional factors. It is also not due to the success of an assimilatory initiative on the part of functionalists. Nor does it derive from self-conscious rapprochement of generativists in the direction of functionalists. Rather, it is an independent development within generative theory, a development that, arguably, coincides with views that functionalists also hold. In this scenario, the Minimalist Program approaches functionalism because, unprovoked by functionalism, generative grammar has discovered the salience to linguistic theory of discourse, language processing, and so forth.

There are also participants in the debate who do not see formalism and functionalism as complementary. In particular, Newmeyer's alignment of the two is controversial. Recall that Hopper objected to what he perceived as unwarranted assimilation of functionalism into formalism. Likewise, Foolen (2002: 99) wrote that for at least some functionalists, 'only a functionalist approach from the beginning to the end can lead to a proper description and explanation'. He went on to quote Langacker's insistence that functional considerations are necessarily foundational, not subsidiary, to the analysis of language. D'Alessandro and van Oostendorp (2017: 3) object that integration of the two into 'a mosaical view' cannot be achieved at present because the two adhere to different definitions of the object of study and rely on different data sources.

Butler spells out a strong anti-complementarian stance in a response to Newmeyer's (2005b) review of Butler (2003): formalism and functionalism are simply incompatible, because 'there is no room in Chomsky's theory, now as in the past, for the view that usage of language is itself a determining factor in the synchronic grammar of a language as well as in the process of language change' (Butler 2006: 205). To illustrate what he sees as the essential incompatibility of formalism and functionalism, Butler drills down on the relation of syntax and semantics. Many, including Newmeyer, have pointed out that throughout the history of a theory dominated by attention to syntax, generativists have in fact assigned various supporting roles for semantics: in Logical Form; in the specification of theta-roles; in the conceptual-intentional system. But to Butler, '[i]n a functionalist account, the claim is not that we can give a semantic interpretation to syntactic phenomena, but that semantics is the driving force, and syntax reflects, at least in part, the meanings that it is there to convey' (p. 208). On this and other bases, Butler denies that formalism and functionalism are converging, or that there are grounds for anticipating convergence.

Participants in the debate between formalism and functionalism have staked out at least these three positions relative to each other. What is surprising is that although the discussion spans contrasting, and strongly held, points of view, exchanges between the two are still relatively sparse. The best sources are texts that expressly contrast the two approaches (e.g., Darnell et al. 1999), and target articles in scholarly journals offset by accompanying peer commentary (e.g., Pinker & Bloom 1990; Newmeyer 1991, 2003 [with commentary surrounding Newmeyer 2005a]; Evans & Levinson 2009 [extending to Rooryck et al. 2010]). Target articles with peer commentary are designed to provoke discordant opinions, which may exaggerate the expression of conflict between formalists and functionalists. Conflict is good and strengthens the discipline, but it also has a polarizing effect, muting points of view that lie between the extremes, and thus may paradoxically increase insularity on both sides.

6.4 Back to Back

There remains an additional juxtaposition of formalism and functionalism. Aligning the two back-to-back calls attention to an important imbalance, namely, that they are not arrayed symmetrically in disciplinary space. Unlike the imaginary conversational partners Forman and Funk, or the interlocutors in Carnie and Mendoza-Denton (2003), real participants in real debates about formalism and functionalism do not hold congruent positions relative to each other. At least in North America and East Asia, formalism is entrenched as the default to which functionalism reacts. In Europe, functionalism has a higher profile, but it still seems to adopt a defensive posture relative to formalism. As evidence for this asymmetry, one notices that remarks about the lack of communication across the two parties are largely made by functionalists (both North American and European), not by formalists. It was a functionalist who asked 'Why Can't We Talk to Each Other?' (Haspelmath 2000), and another who titled an article 'What Formalists Seem Not to Understand About Functionalists' (Nuyts 1986). One can hardly imagine formalists posing Haspelmath's question, or specifying what functionalists do not understand about formalists. Furthermore, functionalists seem to take the presence of formalism for granted in ways that formalists rarely reciprocate. For example, Geeraerts (2010) announces the ascendance of functionalism, but throughout his article keeps measuring that success against the status of generative theory. Moreover, it seems significant that no companion text to Newmeyer (1998) has appeared, in which an avowed functionalist would introduce and explain the debate from a sympathetic but pro-functionalist point of view.

These observations support a sense that, contra Battistella (2000: 431), the tableau is not a simple one in which formalists 'push' and functionalists 'pull'. Rather, formalists occupy a dominant position in the sociology of the field, and do not look over their shoulders anxiously at functionalists. In contrast, functionalists are on guard against their counterparts, expecting to have to argue for the legitimacy of their own views. Comparison of the books by Moro (2016) and by Everett (2012) with which this text began provides an illustration. Moro the formalist brushes away concerns that have absorbed the careers of functionalists in an offhand remark: the capacity of language to transmit meaning and to subserve communication is, to Moro, merely 'trivial' (2016: 2). Everett the functionalist, on the other hand, raises, explains, and responds to a large array of formalist claims, among them the autonomy (or not) of grammar, cognition, and culture; brain specialization and language; the status of recursion and evidence for it in Pirahã; etc.

It is worth adding that, even if this impression of the present-day disposition of formalism relative to functionalism is accurate, it has more sociological than theoretical significance. Formalist versus functionalist tendencies have been in tension for a long time in linguistics; what rises to the surface at any one moment isn't a judgment on its overall adequacy as an account of the nature of language. Other factors affect the bearing of formalism versus functionalism. For example, in the current century, the alliance of formalism with the natural sciences boosts its public profile. Generative formalism has also benefitted from the sustained leadership of a single perseverant, charismatic figure, even acknowledging that not all formalists do align themselves with Chomsky. (A paradox lies here, in that Chomsky has consistently asserted that his ideas represent the views of a tiny minority of linguists [2004: 67–69]—an opinion few observers share.) As opposed to these public-relations advantages enjoyed by formalists, functionalism is very disparate, with no dominant figure, school, or even geographical locale. Functionalism is also averse on principled grounds to the imposition of uniformity. Many of its adherents seem most at home in the relatively private act of collecting, handling, and assessing the actual data of language: one thinks of Halliday's close examination of writers' options for building cohesion in a text, Goldberg's analyses of the many constructions that make up a language, or Langacker's sketches representing his differential breakdown of *kernel of corn* versus *corn kernel*. In contrast, many formalists make claims about language that display counter-intuitive audacity and a willingness to take risks that adds glamour to the public face of the linguist-engineer: the insight that looked beyond the surface of English auxiliaries to recognize abstract patterns of remarkable regularity; Hyams's readiness to impute to pre-schoolers elaborate sensitivity to functional categories; Chomsky's saltationist stance. Juxtaposing the two approaches from diverse angles brings this matter to light, as well as bringing to light more substantive differences between formalism and functionalism.

References

Anderson, Stephen R. (1999). 'A formalist's reading of some functionalist work in syntax'. In Edith Moravcsik, Michael Darnell, Frederick Newmeyer, Michael Noonan, and Kathleen Wheatley (Eds.), *Functionalism and formalism in linguistics*, vol. I (pp. 111–135). Amsterdam/Philadelphia: John Benjamins.

Bates, Elizabeth and Brian MacWhinney. (1990). 'Welcome to functionalism' [Commentary on Pinker & Bloom 1990]. *Behavioral and Brain Sciences* 13: 727–728.

Battistella, Edwin. (2000). [Review of the book *Language form and language function*]. *Journal of Linguistics* 36: 431–439.

Beaugrande, Robert de. (1994). 'Function and form in language theory and research: The tide is turning'. *Functions of Language* 1(2): 163–200.

Bloom, Paul. (1990). 'Syntactic distinctions in child language'. *Journal of Child Language* 17(2): 343–355.

Butler, Christopher S. (2003). *Structure and function: A guide to three major structural-functional theories. Part 1: Approaches to the simplex clause. Part 2: From clause to discourse and beyond.* Amsterdam/Philadelphia: John Benjamins.

Butler, Christopher S. (2006). 'On formalism and functionalism: A reply to Newmeyer'. *Functions of Language* 13(2): 197–227.

Carnie, Andrew and Norma Mendoza-Denton. (2003). 'Functionalism is/n't formalism: An interactive review of Darnell et al. (1999)'. *Journal of Linguistics* 39: 373–389.

Carstairs-McCarthy, Andrew. (1999). [Review of the book *Language form and language function*]. *Anthropological Linguistics* 41: 426–429.

Chomsky, Noam. (1965). *Aspects of the theory of syntax.* Cambridge, MA: MIT Press.

Chomsky, Noam. (2004). *The generative enterprise revisited: Discussions with Riny Huybregts, Henk van Riemsdijk, Naoki Fukui, and Mihoko Zushi.* Berlin: Walter de Gruyter.

Chomsky, Noam. (2005). 'Three factors in language design'. *Linguistic Inquiry* 36: 1–22.

Croft, William. (1995). 'Autonomy and functionalist linguistics'. *Language* 71: 490–532.

D'Alessandro, Roberta and Marc van Oostendorp. (2017). 'On the diversity of linguistic data and the integration of the language sciences'. *Frontiers in Psychology* 8: Article 2002. https://doi.org/10.3389/fpsyg.2017.02002

Darnell, Michael, Edith Moravcsik, Frederick Newmeyer, Michael Noonan, and Kathleen Wheatley (Eds.). (1999). *Functionalism and formalism in linguistics: Volume I: General papers. Vol. II: Case studies.* Amsterdam/Philadelphia: John Benjamins.

Derwing, Bruce L. (1973). *Transformational grammar as a theory of language acquisition.* Cambridge: Cambridge University Press.

Dik, Simon C. (1978). *Functional grammar.* Amsterdam: North-Holland.

Dik, Simon C. (1989). *The theory of functional grammar. Part 1: The structure of the clause*. Dordrecht: Foris.

Enfield, N. J. (2013). 'What I'm reading: Language, culture, and mind: Trends and standards in the latest pendulum swing' [Review of the book *Language: The cultural tool*]. *Journal of the Royal Anthropological Institute* 19: 155–169.

Evans, Nicholas and Stephen C. Levinson. (2009). 'The myth of language universals: Language diversity and its importance for cognitive science'. *Behavioral and Brain Sciences* 32(5): 429–448.

Everett, Daniel L. (2012). *Language: The cultural tool*. New York: Random House.

Fischer, Olga. (2007). *Morphosyntactic change: Functional and formal perspectives*. Oxford: Oxford University Press.

Foley, William A. and Robert D. Van Valin Jr. (1984). *Functional syntax and universal grammar*. Cambridge: Cambridge University Press.

Foolen, Ad. (2002). [Review of the book *Language form and language function*]. *Functions of Language* 9(1): 87–103.

Geeraerts, Dirk. (2010). 'Recontextualizing grammar: Underlying trends in thirty years of cognitive linguistics'. In Elzbieta Tabakowska, Michel Choinski, and Lukasz Wiraszka (Eds.), *Cognitive linguistics in action: From theory to application and back* (pp. 71–102). Berlin: Walter de Gruyter.

Givón, Talmy. (1979). *On understanding grammar*. New York: Academic Press.

Givón, Talmy. (1995). *Functionalism and grammar*. Amsterdam/Philadelphia: John Benjamins.

Goldberg, Adele E. (1995). *Constructions: A construction grammar approach to argument structure*. Chicago: University of Chicago Press.

Golumbia, David. (2008). 'Minimalism is functionalism'. *Language Sciences* 32: 28–42.

Halliday, M. A. K. (2003). 'Systemic grammar and the concept of a "science of language"'. In Jonathan Webster (Ed.), *Collected works of M. A. K. Halliday. Vol. 3. On language and linguistics* (pp. 199–212). London: Continuum. (Original work published 1992)

Haspelmath, Martin. (2000). 'Why can't we talk to each other?' [Review of the book *Language form and language function*]. *Lingua* 110: 235–255.

Hauser, Marc D., Noam Chomsky, and W. Tecumseh Fitch. (2002). 'The faculty of language: What is it, who has it, and how did it evolve?' *Science* 298: 1569–1579.

Hengeveld, Kees. (1999). 'Formalizing functionally'. In Edith Moravcsik, Michael Darnell, Frederick Newmeyer, Michael Noonan, and Kathleen Wheatley (Eds.), *Functionalism and formalism in linguistics*, vol. II (pp. 93–105). Amsterdam/ Philadelphia: John Benjamins.

Hoekstra, Teun and Jan G. Kooji. (1988). 'The innateness hypothesis'. In John A. Hawkins (Ed.), *Explaining language universals* (pp. 31–55). Oxford: Basil Blackwell.

Hopper, Paul J. (1991). 'Functional explanations in linguistics and the origins of language' [Commentary on Newmeyer 1991]. *Language and Communication* 11(1/2): 47.

Hyams, Nina. (1999). 'Underspecification and modularity in early syntax: A formalist perspective on language acquisition'. In Edith Moravcsik, Michael Darnell, Frederick Newmeyer, Michael Noonan, and Kathleen Wheatley (Eds.),

Functionalism and formalism in linguistics, vol. I (pp. 387–413). Amsterdam/ Philadelphia: John Benjamins.

Joos, Martin. (1958). *Readings in linguistics: The development of descriptive linguistics in America since 1925 (2nd ed.)*. New York: American Council of Learned Societies.

Kuno, Susumu. (1987). *Functional syntax: Anaphora, discourse and empathy*. Chicago: University of Chicago Press.

Kuno, Susumu and Ken-Ichi Takami. (1993). *Grammar and discourse principles: Functional syntax and GB theory*. Chicago: University of Chicago Press.

Labov, William. (1987). 'The overestimation of functionalism'. In René Dirven and Vilém Fried (Eds.), *Functionalism in linguistics* (pp. 311–332). Amsterdam/ Philadelphia: John Benjamins.

Langacker, Ronald W. (2008). *Cognitive grammar: A basic introduction*. Oxford: Oxford University Press.

Lass, Roger. (1980). *On explaining language change*. Cambridge: Cambridge University Press.

Moro, Andrea. (2016). *Impossible languages*. Cambridge, MA: MIT Press.

Newmeyer, Frederick J. (1991). 'Functional explanation in linguistics and the origins of language'. *Language and Communication* 11(1/2): 3–28.

Newmeyer, Frederick J. (1992). 'Iconicity and generative grammar'. *Language* 68: 756–796.

Newmeyer, Frederick J. (1998). *Language form and language function*. Cambridge, MA: MIT Press.

Newmeyer, Frederick J. (1999). 'Some remarks on the formalist – functionalist controversy in linguistics'. In Edith Moravcsik, Michael Darnell, Frederick Newmeyer, Michael Noonan, and Kathleen Wheatley (Eds.), *Functionalism and formalism in linguistics*, vol. I (pp. 469–486). Amsterdam/Philadelphia: John Benjamins.

Newmeyer, Frederick J. (2001). 'The Prague school and North American functionalist approaches to syntax'. *Journal of Linguistics* 37(1): 101–126.

Newmeyer, Frederick J. (2003). 'Grammar is grammar and usage is usage'. *Language* 79: 682–707.

Newmeyer, Frederick J. (2005a). 'A reply to critiques of "Grammar is grammar and usage is usage"'. *Language* 81: 229–236.

Newmeyer, Frederick J. (2005b). [Review of the book *Structure and function: A guide to three major structural-functional theories*]. *Functions of Language* 12(2): 275–283.

Newmeyer, Frederick J. (2005c). *Possible and probable languages*. Oxford: Oxford University Press.

Nuyts, Jan. (1986). 'What formalists seem not to understand about functionalists'. *Belgian Journal of Linguistics* 1(1): 225–237.

Payne, Doris. (1999). 'What counts as explanation? A functionalist's account of word order'. In Edith Moravcsik, Michael Darnell, Frederick Newmeyer, Michael Noonan, and Kathleen Wheatley (Eds.), *Functionalism and formalism in linguistics*, vol. I (pp. 137–165). Amsterdam/Philadelphia: John Benjamins.

Pinker, Steven. (1984). *Language learnability and language development*. Cambridge, MA: Harvard University Press.

Pinker, Steven and Paul Bloom. (1990). 'Natural language and natural selection'. *Behavioral and Brain Sciences* 13: 707–727.

Rooryck, J., N. V. Smith, A. Liptak, and D. Blakemore (Eds.). (2010). Special issue on Evans and Levinson's 'The myth of language universals'. [Special issue]. *Lingua* 120(5).

Sampson, Geoffrey. (2005). *The 'language instinct' debate*. London: Continuum.

Tallerman, Maggie. (1998). [Review of the book *Language form and language function*]. *Studies in Language* 24: 423–439.

7 Conclusion

7.1 Engineers and Collectors, Revisited

In this text, we first encountered formalist and functionalist linguistics in two books written for a non-specialist readership. We probed the history of linguistics for earlier attestations of the general orientation of the two approaches, then surveyed varieties of mid-twentieth-century formalism and functionalism up to the present day. Next, we sampled analyses by linguist-engineers versus linguist-collectors on three topics: word order and transitivity in syntax; child language learning; and ideas about the origin of language—analyses which are sometimes coordinate, sometimes in conflict, and sometimes simply discrepant. Finally, we listened to formalists and functionalists talk to each other and talk about each other, and considered their differential status in disciplinary culture. Throughout, the goal has not been to determine the superiority of one side over the other, but rather to understand what makes each distinctive, and what each brings to modern study of language.

This concluding chapter offers two final perspectives on formalism and functionalism. One is inspired by a work of art that captures something essential about formalism; we then turn that image inside-out to imagine a correlative pictorial essence of functionalism. The second compares a matched set of self-representations, by which formalists and functionalists present themselves to the public.

7.2 Portrait of a Linguistic Mindset

An image included in Boeckx's (2006: 96–98) exposition of the Minimalist Program is arresting. Boeckx reproduces three multi-part sets of lithographs created in late 1945 into 1946 by Pablo Picasso, each of which portrays the figure of a single powerful, standing bull viewed from the side and facing to the right. According to Wye (2010: 71–77), Picasso first generated a fully developed image that represented the bull in good anatomic detail, with shadow and shading that gave the figure a plausible three-dimensionality. He then created a second version of the bull that withheld some of that detail, and superimposed on the image a network of lines tracing out what Picasso saw as meridians of tension across the animal's body, diagonally from groin to neck, and arching from the lower back across the flank to the front legs. The third version discarded more of the surface features of the bull's body and limbs to present an increasingly schematic two-dimensional image, with the meridians made more prominent by a sparsity of background detail. The fourth and final version comprised a highly abstract distillation of the shape of the bull: the network of superimposed lines has faded so that what remains is only a sketchy outline of the tail, legs, horns, body, and—Picasso being Picasso—the animal's genitals. He iterated these steps three or four times, so the full collection of Picasso's lithographs captures multiple views of the bull at multiple levels of resolution.

Boeckx sees these lithographs as communicating Picasso's search for the essence of a bull, which he likens to the trajectory of Chomskyan formalism, culminating in the Minimalist Program's search to reduce the whole of a grammar to its sparsest architectural core. That was Pāṇini's aim as well, and a goal that Bloomfield's 'postulates' (1926) approached in a different intellectual-cultural milieu. Moreover, formalism often takes itself as its own object. Pāṇini's *Aṣṭādhyāyī* attracted a large commentarial literature; modern formalist graphic style sublimates language data to attend to its own analysis of underlying human linguistic competence. (Recall Fischer's characterization of formalism: 'the *system* of grammar [is] more important as an object of study than the actual language data'; 2007: 54; emphasis in the original.) About the creation of the bull lithographs, Wye (2010: 15) quotes Picasso as having remarked that 'I've reached the moment . . . when the movement of my thought interests me more than the thought itself'.

Boeckx's (2006) sole concern is formalism, so he does not suggest a functionalist counterpart to Picasso's lithographs. But one can imagine how a functionalist artist working under the motto of 'form follows function' might attempt to represent the essence of a bull. Such an artist might create a multi-layered, multimedia mosaic that collected diverse evidence for the conventional roles of the animal in human culture: close-up images of Spanish bullfighting, registering the views of both participants and opponents; evidence of the worship of sacred bulls in ancient Minoan civilization; data about the commercial value of bulls in agriculture and animal husbandry; a video of Pamplona's 'running of the bulls'; Paleolithic cave drawings of bulls; Arturo Di Modica's 1989 bronze statue 'Charging bull' as a symbol of Wall Street's entrepreneurial spirit; bulls in comparison to their near-relatives water buffalo, bison, domesticated cattle; and so forth. Just as functionalist linguists insist on analyzing non-idealized language as produced by real speakers in real speech contexts, functionalist artists would feature genuine, particularized bulls carrying out conventional activities in their natural milieu. Functionalist artists would, of course, vary in their tactics. Some might organize representations of bulls culture by culture, or distinguish artistic versus scientific representations. Others might extend their work to incorporate the olfactory and kinesthetic traits of bulls: manure; the odor of bovine sweat; the humid, grassy, blast of a bull's breath; the swishing of its tail, its snorting and charging. All this would be brought to bear on how form follows function, for example, how competition among bulls for reproductive opportunities privileges larger body mass; how the high cultural value of a bull makes it the natural centerpiece in Paleolithic art; how human projection of virility to bulls makes their slaughter in bullfighting a paradoxical community-building activity.

Picasso's 'internalist' representation of bulls looks more and more deeply inward, removing successive layers of surface matter to get at the gist of what a bull is. In contrast, our imagined functionalist artist's 'externalist', culturally and physically contextualized representation collects and interprets evidence linking what a bull *is* to what a bull *does*. It is not clear that it would make sense to coordinate these two representations. However, they share a common ambition: to understand the nature of what makes a bull, a bull. Formalist and functionalist linguists both subscribe to that goal with respect to language. The linguist-engineer builds—or distills—a model of the underlying framework of the object of interest, while the linguist-collector assembles samples of that object, and makes sense of those samples with respect to the total collection.

7.3 Formalism and Functionalism Face the World Online

One final perspective on formalism and functionalism turns to how the two represent themselves to the public. Newmeyer (1998) introduces his fictional protagonists 'Sandy Forman' and 'Chris Funk' as graduates of MIT and of the University of California at Santa Barbara, respectively—institutions that Newmeyer doubtless chose for their reputations as polar opposites in orientation. With new insight into the debate between formalism and functionalism, we can analyze how these two prominent American doctoral programs construct their divergent public faces. We will draw as evidence the material posted on their departmental websites assuming that, granted the medium's flexibility and ease of design, texts disseminated on an institutional website have been groomed to accurately depict the group's self-image.

At the top of the homepage of the MIT Department of Linguistics and Philosophy, a brief institutional self-introduction sets the scene:

> Our research aims to discover the rules and representations underlying the structure of particular languages and what they reveal about the general principles that determine the form and development of language in the individual and the species.

> (http://linguistics.mit.edu; accessed 3 August 2018)

Every word of this passage carries strategic weight. The verb *discover* suggests an empirical approach. The expression *rules and representations*, echoing the title of Chomsky (1980), presupposes both that grammar is rule-governed, and that its analysis must consider multiple levels of representation, such as those which (over the history of generative theory) have been variously labeled 'deep structure', 'Logical Form', or 'the external interfaces'. Both those presuppositions are strengthened by the specification that rules and representations 'underl[ie] the structure of particular languages', an expression that admits the existence of abstract levels of language structure beneath an overlying surface.

The text goes on to balance 'particular languages' against 'general principles that determine the form . . . of language'. The existence of those general principles is taken for granted—as signaled by the definite determiner *the* in construction with initial-reference use of the phrase *general principles*—and their first, defining, role is to determine the 'form' of language. (Note also the earlier use of *the* with initial-reference *rules and representations*: the writer presupposes the existence, and obvious relevance to the reader, of 'rules and representations' as well as 'general principles'.) The reference to 'development of language in the individual' registers a role for the study of language acquisition, an issue of long-sustained importance in the generative version of formalism. In the last line, *and the species* may be a shoutout to the recent debate about the origins of language in which generative grammarians have played a leading role.

Perhaps most telling of all, notice that this passage asserts straightaway a central formalist position: that it is 'rules and representations' that determine the form of language. Behind this seems to lie the commitment that it is neither communication, nor cognition, nor culture that imposes a form on language.

In short, this passage posted as if over the doorway into the online presence of linguistics at MIT displays many formalist themes and motifs, and in particular those of generative formalism. The remaining content of the website is consistent with that first impression. In a text reflecting on the department's history, linguistics at MIT is depicted as 'a leading center for research on formal models of human-language phonology, morphology and syntax'. Use of the terms 'formal' and 'model' is salient, as is the absence of reference to domains of human language other than phonology, morphology, and syntax. The next paragraph expands in a similar vein: 'A distinctive feature of the Linguistics Program at MIT has been its insistence on explicit theories of language formalized as grammatical rules and constraints'. In a search of over 8,000 words posted on the website, the word 'function' (or its morphological derivatives) never appears in the sense that contrasts with 'formal'.

Of course, neither Newmeyer's fictional caricature of a new PhD nor a single-sentence summary of something as multifarious as a graduate program does justice to the complexity of the real-life phenomena they stand for. But imagining that 'Sandy Forman' actually had been educated at MIT, the views attributed to Forman in conversation with his counterpart Funk align well with those articulated, and implied, in the institution's website.

Forman's interlocutor, 'Chris Funk', is a graduate of the Linguistics Department of the University of California at Santa Barbara—located geographically on the opposite continental coast, and by reputation intellectually at odds with MIT. The UCSB website's closest analog to MIT's one-sentence institutional self-introduction does not appear on the homepage (www.lin guistics.ucsb.edu/home), but rather in a text linked to the homepage under 'Santa Barbara Sneak Peek':

> The UCSB Department of Linguistics studies the ways that languages and language varieties around the world are used in everyday life. We look to social interaction, social and cultural change over time, and cognitive and biological processes to understand why languages work the way they do. . . . We therefore have a strong commitment to using linguistics to advance social justice as well as scientific knowledge.
>
> (www.linguistics.ucsb.edu/news/announcement/620;
> accessed 4 August 2018)

The hallmarks of functionalism are conspicuous. The department's object of study is not 'language' in the abstract but plural 'language*s*' worldwide; the text further raises the ante to include differential context-dependent manifestations of languages as well ('language varieties'). The target is how languages are 'used in everyday life', obviously invoking functionalist concern with usage. Moreover, the text registers the investment functionalism makes in explanation by listing the top reasons why (from a functionalist perspective) 'languages work the way they do': 'social interaction, social and cultural change . . . and cognitive and biological factors'. Lest any unclarity remain about the orientation of the department to formalism versus functionalism, the passage goes on to mention two long-term goals: first, 'to advance social justice', and secondly—in syntactically subordinate position—'[to advance] scientific knowledge'.

All of the information about linguistics and about graduate study posted on the UCSB website is coherent with the functionalist content of this introductory passage. For example, the value placed on explanation comes up repeatedly: the program 'focuses on the discovery of general, theoretically significant explanations' ('Linguistics—Graduate Program'); 'The . . . faculty share a commitment to asking why languages are as they are. This fundamental question drives the pursuit of functional explanation' ('Research'). The word 'function(al)' appears 13 times in a 4,800-word corpus of the text posted on the website; the word 'form' (in its relevant sense), three times. Arguably, there is also a shadow of the defensiveness that sometimes characterizes functionalist rhetoric. A passage on the homepage declares that:

> As more and more researchers across all fields of linguistics are seeking well-motivated explanations and firmly grounded empirical evidence for claims about the nature of language, UCSB's longstanding leadership in this enterprise puts the department at the cutting edge of linguistic scholarship, developing ideas and methods that are critical for moving the field of linguistics into a new era.
>
> (www.linguistics.ucsb.edu/home; accessed 4 August 2018)

The tone that surfaces here—somewhere between defensive and aspirational—may only communicate context-appropriate self-promotion. But it is salient that, in contrast, the MIT department frames the warrant for its own value point-blank as a long-established fact: 'the Linguistics Program at MIT rapidly acquired an international reputation as a leading center for research' (http://linguistics.mit.edu/graduate/).

A final touch nails in place the orientation of the UCSB department: in the upper right-hand corner of the website's homepage, and repeated as the featured graphic on the department's Facebook page, is a square box in which, in bold upper-case letters and without commentary, appear the words 'FORM FOLLOWS FUNCTION'. In photographs of students and faculty, the same famous aphorism appears inscribed on what seem to be department-issued royal-blue hats.

As we know, the fictional encounter between Newmeyer's Forman and Funk did little to advance their mutual understanding, or even mutual toleration. Some observers believe the two orientations can complement each other; others disagree. But observers, as well as participants who identify as either linguist-engineers or linguist-collectors, can all profit from better insight into what is at stake in the debate between formalism and functionalism.

References

Bloomfield, Leonard. (1926). 'A set of postulates for the science of language'. *Language* 2: 153–164.

Boeckx, Cedric. (2006). *Linguistic minimalism: Origins, concepts, methods, and aims*. Oxford: Oxford University Press.

Chomsky, Noam. (1980). *Rules and representations*. New York: Columbia University Press.

Newmeyer, Frederick J. (1998). *Language form and language function*. Cambridge, MA: MIT Press.

Wye, Deborah and Pablo Picasso. (2010). *A Picasso portfolio: Prints from the Museum of Modern Art*. New York: Museum of Modern Art.

Appendix

Characteristics of Formalism Versus Functionalism

FORMALISM	FUNCTIONALISM
PROFILE, IN SHORT	
Linguist-engineers define inner structure of human language	Linguist-collectors assemble 'cabinets of curiosity'
'Austere, diagrammatic, rule-conscious'	'Loose, approximate, contingent'
Defaults to 'internalist' explanations	'Externalist' explanations
Linguistic competence is central	Attends to linguistic performance
FIELDMARKS	
Embraces abstraction	Deals with particulars, idiosyncrasies
Analyses presuppose, and build, theoretical constructs	Analyses presuppose connection of language, communication, cognition
Searches actively for generalizations	Can be reticent in pursuit of generalizations
Values rigorous formalization of findings	Values fidelity in representing diverse data
States generalizations in absolute terms	States generalizations as statistical probabilities
May admit interaction between formal and functional constraints	Functional forces are a foundational, direct, influence on the shape of language
Pursues narrow range of grammatical facts	Pursues totality of language
'Grammaticality' is a key construct	'Prototypicality' and 'markedness' are key constructs
Language is essentially a vehicle for thought or reasoning, which incidentally plays a role in transfer of information	Language most essentially performs social-interactive functions
Focus on ideal speaker/hearer; postpones or disregards individual variation	Explores individual, group, and community-wide differences

(Continued)

(Continued)

FORMALISM	FUNCTIONALISM
Assumes homogenous speech community	Sensitive to issues of power and solidarity
Distant goal: specify precise contents of human nature	Distant goal: subserve social progress

METHODOLOGICAL PRACTICES; TREATMENT OF DATA

Deductive methods	Inductive methods
Open to bold speculation	Deep analysis of particular cases
Idealized, decontextualized data	Data retain features of natural speech/ text in context
Grammaticality judgments; speakers' intuition and introspection	Case studies; corpora (spoken and textual)
Defining constituency is foundational to analysis	Analysis highlights dependency relationships
Little engagement with written language	Addresses speech/writing differences

ASSUMPTIONS ABOUT THE ORGANIZATION OF GRAMMAR

Assumes autonomy and modularity in organization of grammar	All parts of language are integral to each other
Syntax is an autonomous mental faculty comprising an operational code	Syntax is a tool for encoding meaning, shaped by speakers' intended messages
Sentence is the typical unit of analysis	Highlights discourse
Semantics based on truth conditions	Semantics based on speaker construal
Assumes 'encapsulated' modularity	Semantics/pragmatics form a continuum
Arbitrariness of the lexicon	Champions iconicity, metaphor
Parts of speech are key units: noun; verb; auxiliary; CP; INFL . . .	Grammatical relations are key units: subject; object; topic; theme; focus . . .
Parts of speech resolvable into features	'Fuzzy' distinctions among parts of speech
Categories are sharply delineated, defined by necessary and sufficient conditions	Categorization of elements is subject to gradation: prototypical vs. extended cases

Index